Information Science and Journalism

Information Science and Journalism

A Symbiosis

RABINDRA K. MAHAPATRA
KRUSHNA C. PANDA

RAWAT PUBLICATIONS
Jaipur and New Delhi

ISBN 81-7033-880-8

Published by
Prem Rawat for *Rawat Publications*
Satyam Apartments, Sector 3, Jawahar Nagar, Jaipur - 302 004 (India)
Phone: 0141 265 1748 / 7006 Fax: 0141 265 1748
E-mail : info@rawatbooks.com
Website: rawatbooks.com

Delhi Office
4858/24, Ansari Road, Daryaganj, New Delhi 110 002
Phone: 011-23263290

Typeset by Rawat Computers, Jaipur
Printed at Nice Printing Press, New Delhi

Contents

Preface

The preparation of this academic work has been a long but exciting project intended to be executed as a part of doctoral research. The phenomenon of information presents exciting and far-reaching consequences towards development of this.society. It has entered into every aspect of human lives and their activities. While information fuels social transformation, it affects every body and its role is so pervasive that it has become a common place in the present society. While information has posed challenges and opportunities, it needs to be viewed seriously by the public in general and the professionals in particular in order to know its depth and manifestations to explore the direct benefits for an intellectual mass. Being professionals of Library and Information Science, the authors have tried to explore different areas of information in general and its uses by specific group(s), say, the practicing journalists in particular. Hence, a study of this kind was undertaken to know the contemporary state of information provision available in media centres/ newspaper libraries for the practicing journalists in Orissa along with their seeking behaviour and the type of information they need.

Data for the above study were derived through a pre-ordained questionnaire, from 226 respondents spread over entire state, representing 40 different newspapers of three frequencies in four languages and distributed over eleven different job positions. As a solution to these complex and various job positions, the word 'journalists' has been used inter-changeably with the target respondents consistently throughout the work to avoid any possible confusion.

Journalism is the fourth pillar of democracy. It is the moral responsibility of the libraries attached to various media centres and newspapers to ensure both continuous and free-flow of information to their clientele—the media personnel—including the practicing journalists who play a pivotal role in building a prosperous nation with better informed society. Libraries are meant for the users. If right information does not reach these clientele at the right time, these libraries would fail to justify their very existence. Therefore, this study has become exigent. Though several user studies have been conducted in the recent past by the LIS researchers both at home and abroad, the authors are, however, yet to come across a comprehensive text, exclusively dealing with the newspaper library resources vis-à-vis the information needs of working journalists.

In writing this text, the authors have relied on their varied and continuous experiences as practicing librarians, researchers and teachers of library and information science; besides guiding a few research projects on interdisciplinary topics.

The authors hope, the students and scholars of both the disciplines—LIS and Journalism—will find this text more informative and interesting. Any suggestions for improvement of this volume are essentially welcome and errors, if any, are regretted. This exploratory study, however, provides new directions and basic clues in which the information user research pertaining to working journalists could continue further.

R.K. MAHAPATRA
K.C. PANDA

List of Abbreviations

ABC — Audit Bureau of Circulation

AIR — All India Radio

ARIST — Annual Review of Information Science an Technology

AMRC — Asian Mass Communication Research Centre

CAS — Current Awareness Service

DTP — Desk Top Publication

EIC — East India Company

FIR — First Information Report

GDP — Gross Domestic Product

GNP — Gross National Product

IAC — Information Analysis Centre

IASLIC — Indian Association of Special Library and Information Centres

ICT — Information and Communication Technology

IGNOU — Indira Gandhi National Open University

INFROSS — Information Requirement of Social Scientists

INIS — Information Needs and Information Services in Local Authority Social Services

INSDOC — Indian National Scientific Documentation Centre (it has been changed to NISCAIR)

IR — Information Retrieval

ISB	Information-Seeking Behaviour
IT	Information Technology
LC	Library of Congress
LIC	Library and Information Centre
LIS	Library and Information Science
LISA	Library and Information Science Abstract
NASSDOC	National Social Science Documentation Centre
OCLC	Online Computer Library Centre
OECD	Organisation of Economic Cooperation and Development
OMLINET	Orissa Media Libraries Network
PIL	Public Interest Litigation
PTS	Photo Type Setting
RLIN	Research Library Information Network
RNI	Registrar of Newspapers of India
SDI	Selective Dissemination of Information
UGC	University Grants Commission
UNESCO	United Nations Educational, Scientific and Cultural Organisation
UNI	United News of India
UTLAS	University of Toronto Library Automation System

List of Tables

1

Introduction

A society is a form of congregation where social relationship is, by and large, an essential element to bind the human beings into a common entity. This sort of relationship requires communication either face-to-face between two individuals at the simplest level or among several groups in different forms at a certain complex level. This complexity of communication is, however, desirable while a large number of individuals are closely involved in carrying out certain activities in order to achieve their pre-ordained goals in their respective areas of interest. Such a system of primary communication can be possible through an agency called mass media.

Mass media has not only revolutionised, but also influenced the whole gamut of human activities in a modern society. Its influence on modern social life is so pervasive that it has entered into the very fabric of this society. Thus, it has got adequate potentiality to contribute to an overall development. While the needs of the public are enormous, complex, unlimited and are rapidly increasing day by day, the responsibility of the mass media is growing greater. As a result, mass media has acquired several new dimensions with a view to focus on the most vexing as well as burning social problems of the day.

The media, as an inseparable segment of the society, has a tremendous influence on societal thinking and behaviour. By disseminating information and news, it exercises the cult of a visual society, in which the inner picture of the society is being vividly reflected on its products, i.e., print media, especially newspapers. The process of this media and its activities are centred round the institution called 'press'. Press, in other words, is that social organisation designed to cultivate the communication of information for the masses through a number of print media.

One pledge of crucial interest to the press and all who believe in transparency in governance concerns the right of access to information affecting the people. Although essential to democratic functioning and countering corruption, meaningful legislation to this effect seems to have been either opposed or sabotaged by those in power (Bhattacharjea, 1996: p. 22) on the pretext of official secrecy. For them, the right to hold back information is a facet of power as well as a shield against inquiries into corrupt practices. The right to knowledge and information is an essential prerequisite to the fundamental right to freedom of speech and expression guaranteed under Article 19 of the Constitution of India. Absence of authentic information according to Bhattacharjea (ibid.), however, discouraged informal debate and encouraged wild rumour and speculation, a reference to misleading press reports and misinformation campaigns.

Mere right of access to information is meaningless without the support of an effective communication system to ensure its timely retrieval. Newspaper is, perhaps, one of the most vital and effective mediums through which information on diverse subject fields and public interests reaches a wider spectrum of audience across the country. It is none else, but the journalists, who make this myth into reality through their writings. The working journalists cannot ensure authentic information nor can they improve their writing skill unless their information needs are well taken care of by libraries and information centres through varied documents and other mediums of communication.

However, with the advent of computer and telecommunication technologies, the age-old face-to-face and person-to-person verbal communication monopoly began to perish with a change in the massive movement of information across geographical and language barriers. The industrial revolution saw the light of these modern communication technologies in which new channels were developed, new methodologies were discussed, and new techniques were found out to distribute mass messages as efficiently as possible. A larger system was developed with the growth of both techno-spheres and info-spheres that transform the socio-sphere into a civilised one.

The beginning of the second half of the 20th century, more or less, witnessed the emerging phenomenon of 'communication culture' that builds the modern architecture of the society. A communication channel is more used not only to focus on political, economic and cultural issues in order to reduce poverty, hunger, disease and terrorism, but also to introduce and revitalise peace, harmony, employment, equality of justice and human rights. But one of the most striking features of the communication system is that, from its very inception the entertainment aspect has been given greater importance.

Another important role of mass communication was to provide communication support to the planning, policy making, and inform people about the philosophy and objectives of planning as well as its targets and benefits. The other communicating responsibility is to arouse and involve people by removing their ignorance and superstitions, by changing their negative attitudes, and motivating them into purposeful action. Vidyalankar Committee has stated that the principal aim of communication is to prepare the minds of the people to meet the challenges of these new problems (Malhan, 1990: p. 68). In order to support and complement the objectives of the mass communication system, the print media play a pivotal role, and newspaper becomes the most accepted and highly circulated media of public communication system.

Newspapers take pride of place among these media since they record current information. *Encyclopaedia Americana* (1971: p. 288) defines 'newspaper' as a medium of communication usually published daily or weekly, by which information on current affairs, opinions and entertainment features are circulated among the people. Newspapers have no substitute, because they contain volumes of information, and no other medium, perhaps, can provide such massive and nascent information to users at a time in printed form on daily basis. Again, it can be attributed to the best media that covers different tastes of information to different people such as, prose, poetry, commercial requirements, sports, news and so on. When any reference is required to any new rules and regulations for the public, new plan/proposals, speeches, election results, trade, national defence, arts, music, socio-economic reforms, and a variety of topics of wider interest, it is the newspaper that takes the pride of place. Hence, it has been acclaimed time and again that newspaper is the best and most effective medium of communication with regard to its exhaustive, extensive, nascent, popular and most informative services which it provides to a wider spectrum of audience geographically scattered even in remote and inaccessible areas.

As an agent of mass communication, newspaper is often regarded as the mirror of the society. A contributing agent to the reconstruction of this society, the efficacy of mass communication has undoubtedly a matter of great concern. Commenting on the effectiveness of mass communication, Klapper (1990: pp. 7–8) aptly said:

> The literature has reached that stage of profusion and disarray, characteristics of all proliferating disciplines, at which researchers and research administrators speak wistfully of establishing centres where the accumulating data might be shifted and stored. The field has grown to the point at which its practitioners are periodically asked by other researchers to attempt to assess and cascade, to determine whether we are tumbling, in short, what we know about the effects of mass communication.

The media of mass communication may well exercise extensive social effects upon the masses. They mobilise public opinion and derive a knowledge transformation in the minds of the people. The growing influence of this much debated media has undoubtedly been modified and accelerated by most alluring profession—the journalism—which is closely related to the success of the press, as the true carrier of information and public opinion.

Wainwright (1982: p. 1) aptly remarks: "Journalism is information". To analyse the statement, one can perhaps arrive at the conclusion that journalism is a modern profession, a by-product of technical advancement with main emphasis on the dissemination of information to all.

Journalism is, therefore, a profession meant for people about people. The term, journalism, which is derived from the word 'journal' primarily denotes 'news'. Any publication which is published in a specific periodicity is called journal. A newspaper which is normally published in a specific periodicity, say daily, is the most accepted form of journal. It has been construed that a professional working for the publication of any newspaper is known as a journalist, and the profession proper denotes journalism.

Journalists are those people who are primarily associated with news and views. Their scope of activity is not only limited to the press—the newspapers, but to the whole society to which they serve as their laboratory. The major role played by the journalists in collecting and disseminating information is highly significant and the responsibility entrusted upon the journalists is onerous and remarkable. In bringing the facts to the public, this group of people normally follow a path of truism. To do so, they depend upon the relevance, truth, historical significance, possible causes, and future consequences of the events or facts which they intend to report. In order to collect and establish all these facts of vitality, they apply their intellect, common sense, tact and, wit so as to prove their merits and journalistic talent. In the process, journalists require several information sources including the library and information centre. The succeeding descriptions, therefore, demonstrate the use of such several information sources for their information-gathering activities so as to spell out the relationship between the library and its users—the journalists.

Importance of Library for Journalists

The very efficacy of an activity as profession mostly depends upon some background information or sources that support to prove its vitality. No activity or programme and profession, whatsoever its nature and extent, can flourish without the essence of information of some kind or other. Similarly, journalism as a profession directly deals with the news and views which are highly informative, investigative, and valuable that are amenable to preservation for future reference. This job could effectively be done by an agency, none else, the library.

A library is, therefore, the essence for a journalist. Because, current information is the central to the journalistic activities, as preparation of a feature article or a crucial news item without its proper background information may not only fail to be a foolproof but may make the item even irrelevant and interesting. Providing relevant facts and helping to add background data is the moral responsibility of the libraries. To explore the background, the services of a memory unit, data bank, intelligence unit, or reference section of a library are very much essential for the editorial department of any newspaper establishment (Sindwani, 1979: p. 108). Libraries meant for journalists and associated with any newspaper organisation usually procure relevant information/materials and index them, abstract them or keep them in full text form so as to make them available to their readers on demand.

As the library or information centre is primarily meant for procuring and disseminating information mostly on current topics, it would be of much help to journalists, who often make news as current events or write feature articles, contribute an editorial column, or report an event with its historical background to a newspaper, in all these cases, the library provides a solution. Now, the greater use of libraries by journalists has increased a great deal due to the fact that the job they undertake involves highly thoughtful and hard search compared to any other job. Moreover, the present-day journalism is so highly complex, fluid and controversial that the journalists require some knowledge on almost everything. If the reporting of facts or the historical background of an event proves superficial or wrong, the journalist has to face a defamation suit, causing irreparable loss to his personality and the profession at large. A true public library can save the journalist from such a danger, if he thinks of taking the help of a library before he writes his piece.

In this connection, Lionel Birch (1976: p. 59) while explaining his experience as a journalist, rightly said:

> When I started as a young journalist, I was able to get by with a bit of knowledge about politics, a bit about sport and a bit about something calling society. Today, the young journalists need to know something about sociology, they may even need to have some knowledge on technology, and so on.

This clearly indicates that a journalist is supposed to know something on sciences, social sciences, humanities and his need for a library is a sine qua non phenomenon. This also depicts the magnitude of journalism as a profession, which has undergone a sea change in recent years.

There are different dimensions of library use by different types of journalists. The purpose and extent of use of a library by editorial staff may not be the same as that of the reporting staff of any newspaper establishment. Similarly, the information requirements of a press photographer (photo journalism), an economic/financial reporter, a political correspondent would still and bound to be different from each other. The editorial department under the leadership of the news editor often seeks to use the library for a variety of information needs and guidance. Original news items from the teleprinter printout in which the material covering the news may be too brief and without any background information. In such a situation, the editorial staff usually step into a library to consult the relevant reference materials and newspaper clippings for further background information in order to strengthen the viability of the news that makes it most interesting, factual and informative.

While reporting about natural catastrophe, fatal accidents, brutal murder, report-making on election results, corrupt electoral practices, and misdeeds of prominent personalities, it is essential on the part of the editorial staff to cite some of the similar events which have taken place earlier and the remedial measures or judicial strictures, if any, issued to that effect. The library indeed plays a significant role for such contribution to news-making in order to make the same more reliable, trustworthy, interesting, besides adding value to the news content.

Journalistic writings are more of a literary nature. Most of the editorial staff require to develop and improve their skill in the respective language in which the newspaper is published. The knowledge of English in particular is a sine qua non to become a good editorial staff, as because, the original news items obtained through the teleprinter are often transmitted in English language. In order to make the news items readable, the editorial staff must reshape these as per the required standard. In this regard, the use of reference tools like language dictionaries, subject dictionaries, biographical dictionaries and gazetteers are very often essential. Sometimes, the journalists also require to consult a number of standard books that prescribe the techniques and guidelines as to how best reporting and editing could be made. This is particularly helpful for the new entrants in the profession. To do so, they either run to a library available in the near vicinity or depend upon the library attached to their own newspaper establishments for consultation and reference. Thus, it is an established fact that without sufficient and relevant information from the library, the news items often remain incomplete and without library, the efficiency and effectiveness of the editorial staff in particular can hardly be expected.

The library has also a greater role to play in providing information needed for the journalists working as correspondents and reporters. While collecting news from the field, they use to analyse the particular item with its background information with retrospective effect so as to make the news more interesting, readable and acceptable by a wider audience. That background information with detailed analysis can be had either from the library attached to the parent newspaper establishment or from the local library. The reporter, while preparing his story, usually keeps in constant touch with the library in order to check the validity of facts and statements to be reported. Besides, he avails himself of the press clipping services and ascertains background history from several relevant tools such as gazetteers, census reports, commission reports, and outstanding theories on the subject.

Journalists, who are particularly writing feature articles and having specialisation in it, are often proved to be the most potential users of the library. Because, feature writing by nature needs detailed account of the subject in which the journalists intend to contribute. In the process, they have to acquire many things such as, information that has been published earlier on the subject, original reports, research work undertaken and its results, speeches of leaders, specialists, government publications denoting the official policy, etc., are very much vital before starting to write an article. The role of the library in identifying and disseminating information on all these aspects is really remarkable.

Special correspondents of the newspapers are those journalists who are specialised in specific subject fields on which they report. The nature of their job compelled them to abstain from frequent library use. They normally use their own special records for compilation of reports. Despite this, special correspondents, however, use library materials to update their knowledge in the specific subjects as well as in preparing the news-reports on current items of wider interest. Thus, the foregoing facts clearly depict that while good libraries are required for good and qualitative journalism, good and effective media becomes imperative to make the library more functional. The importance of a library to journalists, therefore, can hardly be questioned.

Background of the Study

Libraries appear not only as source of information, but also as a way of life for those who devote their profession and valuable time for research and generation of creative and intellectual thoughts. Journalists are usually categorised as those professionals and persons directly related to the process of knowledge-generation. Besides, there are other potential readers, active researchers, writers, scientists and veteran social reformers, who by their writings also actively participate in the knowledge-generation process. The process of their professional activities is too much inclined towards the use of information, its resources and the place where those valuable and relevant information, literature and documents are permanently located—libraries.

Libraries are, therefore, the outcome of the social milieu and a necessity in most countries. They represent a major store-house of human knowledge. Their values rest not merely on their facility to store information, but also on their capability to effectively disseminate it in optimum quality and quantity to any information-seeking community.

Libraries stand as a vital source of information and as an invaluable adjunct to the print media, i.e., press. The effectiveness of the press largely depends upon the efficient and well-organised library services. Just as the effectiveness of a corporate body's business mostly depends upon the right information at a right point of time from a system for its decision-making, similarly, the successful functioning of the press largely relies upon information and how well it is organised and efficiently disseminated in its library. Deficiency of right information to the right media person at the right time may, therefore, lead to severe loss to the quality of news generation.

Library is considered as the memory of the newspaper and consequently, the memory of the community it serves. The services it provides to the journalists directly, is the services it renders the whole newspaper-user community. From this, the magnitude of the library's place in the press world can easily be presumed.

The well-organised news library of a daily newspaper undoubtedly plays a crucial role in the production of news. Ward, Hansen and Mclead (1988: p. 146), therefore, have rightly said that, the library is the path that reporters and editors routinely take as they conceptualise, develop, write, and edit the day's news. It is thus an acknowledged fact that a good library is the source of a good newspaper, and a journalist keenly using the library can enrich himself and can effectively serve the media for a better society.

The present problem of the existing newspaper and other media libraries in the country and their use by the journalists is far from satisfactory. Journalists, irrespective of their qualification, experience, level of intellect, critical and investigative bent of mind, are required to use libraries, because, they need to improve the quality of their news in respect of content, currency, relevance and authenticity. But, the situation often remains quite unfavourable to them, as there are hardly good newspaper libraries with adequate resources to serve their journalists. If at all, the libraries are existing within the premises of concerned newspaper organisation, such libraries are either small with meagre resources and inadequate reference support or no information services are provided.

While explaining the condition of such newspaper libraries in Calcutta, Chatterjee (1977: p. 152) aptly remarks:

> While there are no libraries at all in many units, the stocks are not properly classified and catalogued in most of the existing ones. There is no exhaustive and comprehensive clipping and indexing services available in any of the libraries. The enormous research potentiality of the newspapers virtually remains untapped. Evidently, the libraries are unable to play the role that they should play. The main reasons for this condition are, non-availability of required space, staff and, of course, finance.

This more or less applies to the present scene of newspaper libraries in the country. The libraries that play a major contributing role to news-making has not yet been properly realised by the media persons, especially the newspaper owners who are to take interest in developing libraries in their respective newspaper organisations.

Similar is the attitude of the working journalists towards libraries in their respective newspaper organisations. Most of them hardly realise the importance of information available in the library that can enrich and strengthen the news items with much background and relevant information. While some journalists do not feel the necessity of giving much background information to their news, perhaps, owing to their sheer negligence, others become victim due to their mere ignorance. The most common complaint against Indian newspapers is that their stories often lack background information. They generally assume that readers are well informed on the subject. The correct attitude according to Parthasarathi (1984: p. 94) is, perhaps, to provide a meaningful background and explanation for every story they contribute.

Indian journalists are not very keen on using several information sources before preparing a news item. Parthasarathi (ibid.), therefore, has pointed out further:

> Reports put out by news agencies are finished products when they reach the sub-editor and do not need much further editing except condensation and weeding out verbose but even they are very often careless in spelling and grammar, and in idiomatic usage. Sub-editors, it is well-known, are not too fond of dictionaries, because they consider it a waste of time to refer to it everything they come across, a new word whose meaning and spelling they do not know and they would rather give the benefit of doubt to the writer, that is, the reporter.

Journalists are also not adequately conscious about the use of libraries and its several services for the cause of their reporting and news preparation. This can be attributed to the deplorable state of affairs for the standard of newspapers in India. While India, according to an estimate, occupies fourth position in the publication of daily newspapers in the world, it can be assumed that the number of working journalists associated with the print media is quite considerably more. The profession of journalism has been accepted as an elite and noble profession. But, the professionals who are coming under 'working journalists'* are

---

* The phrase 'working journalist' according to Press Council of India (1954) refers to only those whose professed avocation and the principal means of livelihood is journalism should be regarded as working journalist.

still lagging behind in respect of their practice of information-use.

The situation in the state of Orissa is not different from the national scene. With the growth of newspapers, particularly the dailies, the professional journalists working in various newspaper organisations are increasing day-by-day in the state. They seem to have been highly influenced by the professional cult, modern technology, increasing organisational attributes, specialised education, technique of mass communication, and increased sense of social responsibility. But it is not exactly known about their sense of attitude and awareness towards libraries, information services and systems. In order to develop their journalistic standards, to equip them with the present situation and the latest trend, it is highly essential to make a study of the information needs and information-seeking behaviour of these working journalists in the state. Such a study is usually undertaken by the Library and Information Science scholars who can better identify the problems associated with the profession of journalism and can suggest possible solutions for improving the standard of existing library services by bringing suitable changes to the existing information systems to be tailored to the information needs of the journalists and other media persons.

The existing literature on the subject has, however, clearly depicted that no such exclusive study has yet been undertaken at the Ph.D. level in the country on the reading habits, information needs and seeking behaviour of the working journalists.

This emphasises that there is an urgent need to examine the utilisation of the existing library resources and facilities by the journalists and to collect more information concerning the way they seek and approach information from an information system.

The present study undertaken in the state of Orissa has, therefore, become essential and its outcome would be more or less a replica for the other states as well as for the whole journalist community, as most of the attributes are likely to remain common representing their professional character in seeking information and utilisation of varied library resources. This study, therefore, merits immediate attention of journalists, newspaper management, various news agencies, library and information scientists, policy-makers and other media establishments in the country so as to bring suitable reforms in the existing library and information systems tailored to the needs of the media persons in general, and the working journalists in particular.

Statement of the Problem

The present study entitled *Information Science and Journalism* is a topic of great significance and interest not only to the scholars of LIS, but also to the information society as a whole. Working journalists in particular, who occupy a place of eminence in the society and shoulder the responsibility of reforming the society and nation-building through their writings, constitute a dynamic and potential group of library and information-users. They are charged with the duty of translating the whole public life of mankind. Having been entrusted with such a heavy task and a great social onus, the working journalists need to maintain a sound communication order in the society. This phenomenon gives rise to the provision of supporting services to enhance their professional standard and to improve their writing skill.

Thus, the support of libraries and information services to ensure a free flow of information to improve journalistic activities has become exigent. Then a spontaneous urge comes about the need for assessing the status of the working journalists, the way they use the libraries, the manner in which they seek information, their use-pattern, and their behaviour towards the information system, information sources and services they use, etc., as those would be of immense help for the librarians, library administrators, and the planners of media libraries to revamp their library and information systems according to the information requirements and reading tastes of the working journalists.

The library and information scientists in their respective subject fields have undertaken user studies of several kinds. However, study on information needs and information-seeking behaviour of working journalists in Orissa, still remained unexplored. Moreover, user studies have become very popular among LIS scholars and librarians so as to trace out the information requirements of a particular group or class of users of a given library or information centre within a given geographical area. This area of study is found to be the most useful in a successful and challenging career in LIS.

In addition to this, the present study also intends to identify the status and position of working journalists in Orissa, their educational attainments, professionalism, research activities in journalism and mass communication, and the available information resources so as to assess the future requirements. In the process of making an overview of the journalism profession in Orissa, the present study also aims to highlight some of the key issues responsible for bringing the existing media libraries to a state of sombre. This, in fact, would help to identify the factors responsible for the growth and development of journalism in the state along with other attributes required to assess the problems and prospects of the whole spectrum of information systems and services required by the working journalists in particular.

Therefore, the present study is an attempt to make an in-depth analysis of various information requirements and reading interests of working journalists, their approach to information, and the existing library facilities available to them in the state of Orissa which has yet remained unexamined and unexplored.

Scope and Limitations of the Investigation

Every study has two vital constraints—the theme and finance. This ultimately compels a social researcher to limit the scope of his investigation to make the study more precise, specific, and time-bound.

The present study is thus a form of user study designed to bring within its confines only the working journalists of Orissa, their information requirements, information-seeking behaviour, their approach to varied information sources and channels, their awareness towards myriad information systems and services, their reading habits, and the existing library facilities available to them in the state. How information becomes an effective factor for the development of the journalists is the primary concern of the present study. This is because, journalism and information are symbiotic. But how much influence information has inflicted upon journalism has never been properly assessed neither by the journalists nor by the scholars of LIS. By undertaking this study in a developing state like Orissa, the present investigation primarily aims to establish the phenomenon of 'information needs' of the working journalists in different ramifications, besides identifying their status, educational attainments, professionalism, and research activities in the field of journalism and mass communication.

Further, the present work is restricted exclusively to the working journalists in Orissa, those who are making their contributions to various leading Oriya dailies/newspapers.

Thus, the scope and limitation of the present study can be summarised as under:

1. the present study considers only the working journalists in Orissa as its sample respondents (i.e., limitation of respondents by class);
2. it includes only those working journalists who have been contributing to daily newspapers in Oriya and English published and circulated in Orissa (i.e., limitation by class and language of newspapers they represent);
3. it includes those journalists who are not only working on regular payment basis with newspapers, but also regularly contributing to the newspapers on a freelance basis, i.e., freelance journalists (i.e., limitation of respondents by the type of job they hold);

4. it includes only those working journalists who have been residing within the territorial jurisdiction of Orissa (i.e., limitation by geography); and
5. this study has included all categories of working journalists having different job positions irrespective of their age, sex, qualification, remuneration/salary and the newspaper they represent, but excludes the teachers in journalism and retired journalists (i.e., limitation by category of respondents).

Thus, the sample in the present study remains confined only to working journalists including freelancers, who continue to work with different newspaper organisations and regularly contribute to newspapers, especially the daily ones. The retired journalists, teachers, students of journalism and mass communication are, however, excluded from the scope. Although the present study did not initially consider the age factor of the respondents, still the collected sample found to have been attributed to the age range of 25 to 60 years for those respondents, included in the study.

Objectives of Investigation

This study is primarily designed to reflect the reading habits, information needs, seeking behaviour, and the use-pattern of the varied information sources and channels by the working journalists in Orissa. Besides, it analyses the way the working journalists approach information, their knowledge about varied information sources and channels; and the existing library facilities made available to them.

The present study, therefore, sets forth the following objectives:

1. to find out the relative importance of varied information sources consulted by the working journalists included in the survey;
2. to find out the nature and degree of constraints experienced in the process of information-seeking by the working journalists;

3. to discover the principal information needs and resources utilised for obtaining the desired information by the them;
4. to assess the extent of their knowledge and co-operation prevailing among themselves relating to their day-to-day information needs;
5. to examine the limitations, if any, of the existing library facilities and services made available to them;
6. to examine their approaches to varied information sources and/or for locating the information in-need;
7. to ascertain both strengths and weaknesses of the collections of the respective media and services on which they depend;
9. to find out the latest trend relating to the nature of search strategy employed by the working journalists for the current information as well as for obtaining references;
10. to ascertain the extent of their awareness and knowledge concerning to various services in their respective field of interests made available to them by different libraries and information centres both in and out of the state;
11. to find out the various types of documentary sources used by them and the degree of their dependence on libraries;
12. to identify the quantum of time spent by them in reading and scanning the literature in the field of journalism and mass communication relevant to their profession;
13. to investigate their habit of subscribing to journals (both current and retrospective) as well as newspapers;
14. to find out explanation of observed phenomena and prediction of behaviour;
15. to evaluate the overall existing information environment prevailing for the working journalists in Orissa and to find out the ways and means for a better information-related situation for their working conditions and career; and finally
16. to provide clues for solution of any/or all of these problems of their knowledge updating through a chain of libraries so as to make the library system more meaningful, effective, and a viable service institution for the cause of journalism.

Review of Literature

An enthusiastic research beginner, in spite of his/her subject affiliation, is required to go through the research findings of similar work(s), if any, done previously. Such an exercise seems to be a boon for the scholar not only to carry out his research work more scientifically and efficiently, but it also adequately guides the scholar from where to start and how to start the present research, besides reflecting the trend of the subject and helping to check the duplication of the efforts.

However, literature on "Information Science and Journalism" is not very replete. Having surveyed a number of available sources—both printed and electronic databases—it is found that there are very scanty research works and publications on journalists' use of libraries in general and their information-seeking behaviour in particular. In India, research works undertaken by library and information scientists on journalism and mass communication is also not very much encouraging as very little effort has been made by the LIS scholars in this direction. Surprisingly, a subject of such magnitude still remains unexplored. Hence, the present study became necessary.

The study undertaken by Rosamma Joseph in Kerala on "Information Needs of Newspaper Organisations and Journalists' Use of Libraries" shows that the trend of using libraries by the journalists is not so much encouraging. Journalists use libraries mainly for the background materials and for obtaining specific items of information. The information that journalists obtain from libraries are used mainly for writing features, articles, news items and for editing news items. Her study has identified further that journalists prefer to consult more informal sources of information rather than using the libraries in a desired manner as researchers use.

The findings of the work "Information-Seeking Behaviour and the Perceptions of Information Channels by Journalists of Two Daily Newspapers" by Nancy Lee Herron has revealed that newspaper journalists surveyed prefer informal channel-use over formal channel-use two to one, and that personal communication especially with colleagues was found to be the most important factor across all six principal areas of journalistic specialty. While journalists were relatively consistent on their use of the various source types, there was diversity in the way, the different types of journalists look for and use varied information sources. Although reliability of channel and source types use was perceived to be important to journalists, the extent of use of a library and its accessibility tend to affect the frequency of use.

The study done by L. Hoglund on "Media and Communication" enumerates some current research projects wherein the role of the library in higher education, especially for the community of journalists, in determining their information needs is described.

U.S. Eden, in his study on "Information, Needs and Information-Seeking Behaviour Patterns of Journalists in Nigeria" has clearly depicted specific areas of information needs and information-seeking behaviour patterns of journalists in selected Nigerian towns, formal information sources consulted and the role of libraries and librarians in the media organisations in the concerned areas.

The research project undertaken by C. Baggs on "Information Needs and Patterns of Information-Seeking Behaviour of Journalists and Researchers in the National Media, Wales: A Study" focuses on the assessment and evaluation of information needs and researchers engaged in the Wales national media and the current pattern of information-seeking behaviour among them.

In the process of literature search, the investigator tried to collect literature available on the subject comprehensively. It was found that only three articles that are of most relevant to this study are of in Czech language which could not be obtained in translated form in English inspite of the best efforts. However, the work of Jan Bartak as "Journalists, Their Information

Requirements and How to Meet Them", Samuel Brecka's work as "Users of Information in Journalism" and Jiri Cepak's work on "Some Problems Concerning for the Design of an Automated Information System for Journalists and its Realisation", etc., are some of the useful studies which too remained unavailable for review.

Hypothesis and Methodology

An analytical approach to information needs and information-seeking behaviour of working journalists will provide a straight breakthrough not only in their information-use pattern, but will also help to develop a system approach to need-based information for their career and working environment. The present study is based on the premise that study on "Information Science and Journalism" determines the information needs of journalists and helps in designing the information systems and services.

Hypotheses

However, hypotheses formulated for the present study are as follows:

1. the job of a journalist involves a considerable degree of intellect and academic background;
2. journalists used to spend a considerable period of time in the library to increase their habit of consulting myriad information sources for developing their writing skills and journalistic activities;
3. journalists are not ordinarily amenable to current information services for their professional acumenship; and
4. journalists use frequently to those information sources from libraries that are directly related to their profession.

The present study perhaps would be a boon for not only revamping the existing library and information sources made available to the working journalists, but will also be a guideline for developing an information system for journalism and mass communication activities.

Methodology

Since the primary goal of the present study is to identify the key factors associated with the information needs and information-seeking behaviour, and the use-pattern of information of the working journalists in Orissa, first, the different newspaper organisations existing in the state are identified and a list of journalists working with them including the freelancers are collected from these organisations for the purpose of the sample.

A structured questionnaire, with both closed and few open options, was administered to elicit both quantitative as well as qualitative information from the respondents relevant to the study in the light of their observations and experiences. The relevance and utility of each item was also carefully examined before their inclusion in the questionnaire.

After obtaining the address of the each journalist from the Department of Information and Public Relations, Government of Orissa and from the different newspaper organisations, the said questionnaires were mailed by post to the working journalists and some were delivered in person, particularly to those available within the capital city of Bhubaneswar. A personal request was made to the respondents as and when the investigator met them for early return of the filled-in questionnaire. Some respondents desired that the investigator should sit before them to get the questionnaire filled-in, perhaps owing to the technicalities of the questionnaire from information science perspective. The respondents to whom questionnaires were mailed by post were again reminded by a letter for an early despatch of filled-in questionnaires. As it was initially decided to study around 500 journalists, 490 printed questionnaires were sent, out of which only 226 filled-in questionnaires were received back by the investigator, thus having response rate of only 46 per cent.

The data collected through questionnaires were then scrutinised and their consistency was checked before analysis.

Scheme of the Work

The whole gamut of the present study is divided into nine broad chapters covering the wide spectrum of informational and behavioural aspects of working journalists and their professional interaction with library and information systems available to them.

The chapter 1 is introductory. It provides a detailed background justifying the need for the investigation. Some of the vital miens discussed in this chapter are: importance of library to journalists, a brief background of the study, the statement of the problem, scope and limitations of the investigation, a short review of literature, hypotheses formulated and methodology adopted, the scheme of the work, and finally, the constraints encountered in the process of investigation.

The chapter 2 is the literature on user studies and how it takes into its ambit the subject of LIS. It depicts clearly the conceptual framework of user studies, its genesis and development, a taxonomical division of users and user studies, the different methods and techniques employed in conducting user studies, the trends and models of user studies including a vivid scenario of research on user studies in India.

The chapter 3 reflects the literature relating to information, its basic concept, definition, and its significance to LIS. This chapter also presents a vivid description and analysis of information, its concept, various characteristics, types, principles, qualities, and information channels.

Information needs as a concept in the LIS scenario has been vividly described in the chapter 4. The chapter 5 discusses in detail the concept of information-seeking behaviour, which is the central phenomenon of this study and its related areas. Taking consideration of the new emerging technology, the chapter 6 has been given that discusses in brief the use of information and communication technologies in journalism and mass communication.

The chapter 7 seems to be a vital one as it deals with journalism in Orissa and the role of journalists towards the development of society in general, and the newspaper in particular. This chapter also discusses the importance of libraries and information centres for the improvement of journalism and mass communication profession in the country with specific reference to Orissa.

The chapter 8 reflects analysis and interpretation of data including some of the vital findings of the present investigation. The chapter 9, the last one, presents a precise conclusion and some feasible suggestions, which the investigator feels necessary to incorporate.

Constraints

The investigator has experienced a lot of difficulties and constraints during the course of present investigation. More serious among them are discussed hereunder.

As the investigator has certain interest in journalism and mass communication, a topic of such magnitude was decided for research in consultation with the research supervisor and some of the working journalists known to the investigator in order to elicit their views and suggestions before taking up such an arduous work. Surprisingly, some of the working journalists, who have been consulted by the investigator, though expressed the proposed work to be a good one of high research value, and assured their help in the matter, the investigator did not receive their cooperation in a way the same was assured and expected.

In course of distribution and collection of filled-in questionnaires back from the respondents, the investigator had to sustain a great loss of energy, money and valuable time by visiting the journalists frequently, deputing representatives to them at given intervals, reminding repeatedly through several telephone calls, letters and through other modes of request which, however, did not serve the purpose of getting back the whole filled-in questionnaires from the respondents. Such a tendency ultimately led to a meagre response rate of only 46 per cent.

The investigator had to encounter an equal number of problems relating to collection of literature on the subject. He had to visit some national-level information centres like Indian National Scientific Documentation Centre (INSDOC), National Social Science Documentation Centre (NASSDOC), some special libraries and information centres like Indian Institute of Mass Communication (IIMC), National Council of Educational Research and Training (NCERT), British Library, American Centre Library, and few newspaper libraries, such as, *Times of India*, *The Hindustan Times*, *Indian Express* etc., all located in New Delhi. The investigator had also visited some university libraries to collect literature and other material relevant for this study as the same was not available in the local libraries. Besides this, some university libraries like SNDT, Calicut and an international institute like Asian Mass Communication Research Centre (AMRC), Singapore were also contacted for obtaining relevant information.

In the process, the investigator consulted Library and Information Science Abstract (LISA) abstracts and several other databases so as to identify the related research work, if any, done on the subject. Unfortunately, there was no such exclusive work done by LIS professionals/scholars on the information needs and information-seeking behaviour of the working journalists in English language. Only three articles were found in Czech language which again could not be translated into English in spite of the best efforts made by the investigator. Owing to non-availability of translation facilities, such a situation rendered the literature review far from expectations.

These constraints to some extent have affected the results of the study notwithstanding the best of efforts made by the investigator. However, against all odds, the present work was done with the active, positive and ungrudging support of the research supervisor who has done everything possible to complete the work in the scheduled time frame. The succeeding chapters will show different aspects of the subject matter and the extent to which it could fulfil the expectation of the target audience.

2

Information-User Studies

Information is a vital resource. In the present era of information explosion, publication deluge, literature flood, and technological revolution, it has been increasingly felt in library circles that the better the services to users, the greater would be the organisational satisfaction. This is simply because, a library being a service institution is meant for users irrespective of their magnitude and desire. It is, therefore, necessary that the information generated at any point and on any subject be acquired, processed, organised, and be disseminated expeditiously to its appropriate users for their optimum use. User studies, therefore, over the years have attempted to explain the information-use phenomena, information-use behaviour, and information-use control and improvement in all its ramifications and essential conditions.

Thus, thorough knowledge about the users and their information needs is a pre-requisite for planning, organisation, and development of any library and information system. Studies about users and their information needs have, therefore, become imperative not only on the part of the LIS scholars, but also on the part of policy-makers, planners and library administrators.

Most of the professionals today would agree that a library in its true sense, irrespective of its type and location, is neither judged by its magnificent building, nor by its huge collection, large human force, and still not by its rich fiscal resources but by its use. Because, the proper use of a library involves a number of issues, viz., use, non-use and misuse. With the pace of time, there is a spectacular change in the concept of information-use in the recent past and the role of library has undergone sea changes.

Initially, libraries were established primarily to make people aware about their documents and the type of information available. However, the real concept of library use as a part of library and information system emerged later owing to several factors, such as manifold increase in the rate of literacy and book production, information explosion and publication deluge, enactment of public library laws in different states in systematising their library services, emergence of interdisciplinary subjects, improvement in library techniques and procedures in bringing simplifications in the existing library systems, and rapid entry of computer and telecommunication technologies into the threshold of libraries, and many more.

Dr. S.R. Ranganathan, while formulating the five laws of Library Science, first published in 1931, had given immense importance to the use factor. His first law "Books are for use" followed by other four laws tremendously signifies the real concept of document/information-use by the user. Inspite of Dr. Ranganathan's message to library world to keep "use of information" and their user in mind while developing a library and information centre and its services, the library planners and administrators have hardly paid any attention in this respect, especially in India until the beginning of the 1960s. The efforts in the past were mainly in the direction of initiation of freshers on the use of large university or special libraries, only as a part of their reference work. The last two decades, however, have witnessed commendable changes in the phenomenon of information-use and control, whereby a good number of studies on "information-use" have been attempted by LIS professionals and researchers alike, so as to bring suitable reforms in the library systems and services in order to make the library more purposive, and user-friendly.

There are no generally accepted definitions on use studies (Javelin and Repo, 1952). However, a library-use study is defined as any study that deals with the use of library, in any or all of its aspects, by its patrons or its staff (Tobin, 1974: p. 101). These studies are primarily conducted to improve the existing conditions of the library systems and services. While users constitute one of the most significant trio of the library system, all directions towards improvement of a library system mostly concentrate upon them. Recognising the impact of the users towards the development of libraries, researchers, however, gradually become active and more inclined to undertake user studies. The use studies, as indexed in library literature, basically involves the study of one or three possible types of patrons. They include: (i) individual users, (ii) specific group of users, and (iii) non-users. Of the 477 use studies indexed, 340 (71%) were focussed on individual users, followed by 132 (27%) studies on specific group of users, and only 5 (1%) of them are on non-users.

In a library and information environment, the term 'user' becomes one of the most prominent terminologies on which, the very existence of the whole library system depends. If one asks "What for the collection?" "For whom the library is meant?" "Why so much furniture?" "Why cataloguing...classification to be done?" "Why so much information services are to be undertaken in the library?" The only answer to all these questions is perhaps, the 'users'. It is, therefore, more transparent that the whole spectrum of the library system is directed towards users. Unless a given library system assesses the actual information requirements of its potential users and understands their reading tastes so as to make the library user-friendly and purposive, the whole efforts and energy employed in building up the library becomes futile. In order to create a good library and information environment to make the library services more effective and meaningful to the tune of its target audience, library researchers have now started their research activities more towards users and their needs, than any other field of librarianship. Such research activities are often termed as 'user studies', the concept of which has been dealt more lucidly in the succeeding paragraphs.

User Study: A Conceptual Framework

A librarian is usually responsible to answer certain crucial questions relating to library's effectiveness, choice and suitability of library material, library's collection, the degree of use and non-use of library material and services, and the extent to which the users are satisfied with the library services. Professionals would, therefore, agree that thorough knowledge about the users and their information needs is a pre-requisite for planning any library system. Thus, studies about users and their information needs are becoming imminent on the part of library policy-makers, planners and administrators. Such studies which fall under the ambit of LIS research are popularly termed as 'user studies' (Subramaniam, 1983: p. 200).

The role of the library as a social and service institution fulfilling the information needs of the society for its upliftment as a whole is being widely recognised world over. Although librarian's role is not underestimated, he is primarily concerned with the needs of the users for whom the whole concept of the library exists. User studies are, therefore, seldom considered as stigma of library usage.

Realising the magnitude of the concept 'user study', several information researchers/scientists have defined this phrase in their own ways. To Girija Kumar (1989: p. 253), the phrase 'user studies' refers to the diagnostic studies for discovering the casual relationship between the user of information, and the information system. User studies according to Lahiri (1990: p. 337), however, are often instigated as attempts to understand, to justify, to explain or to expand library usage and consequently, to gain more knowledge about the process of communication concerning their libraries and their respective clientele. Sangameswaran and Gopinath (1987: p. 142), however, have expressed a different denotation of the concept of 'user studies'. According to them, the user studies are hardly restricted to actual or potential users alone, as several such studies have also been made of non-users, who are said to constitute nearly 70 per cent of the population even in a developed country like, USA.

User studies, in fact, were originated with the perception that by understanding users' need and information use, one could design an effective information system. Today, user studies are well refined using more sophisticated sociological techniques and focussing more on system-oriented studies as background research is primarily related to cognition and behaviour (Dhawan and Sachdeva, 1987: p. 103).

Why of User Studies?

The question as to why user studies are necessary, remains mostly undebated among the scholars. Without providing satisfactory reasons for conducting user studies, it seems the study would remain incomplete. The reasons for conducting user studies are varied and many. The following are some of the important reasons for which user studies are undertaken in libraries and information centres:

1. to know the users and their information needs;
2. to identify the levels and kinds of user needs;
3. to identify the approach, perception and information-seeking behaviour of users in the parent library environment;
4. to identify, by the results, the real strength and weaknesses of the existing library resources and services;
5. to specify the limitations or problems which might appear to discourage the use of the library;
6. to understand the level of involvement and participation of the users in building a good library environment; and
7. to improve the library system as a whole.

On the other hand, Sangameswaran (1987: p. 142) foresees five vital reasons that make user studies exigent. They include: (i) to identify the potential users and to categorise them; (ii) to identify their information requirements by the class of information needed and the level and type of communication media required; (iii) to identify the existing resources and services so as to achieve comprehensiveness of information even without unwanted duplication of efforts and finances; (iv) to evaluate various existing services in relation to their utility to their users so as to effect suitable modifications and to introduce new services as and when necessary; and (v) to achieve overall improvements in the parent library system from the feedback obtained.

The foregoing reasons are quite pragmatic in achieving the preordained goals of a given library system of any class, and to make the library environment more user-friendly and purposive. The basic necessity of undertaking such a study on users is to know who are they, what are their information requirements, and what are suitable methods available to provide need-based services to derive their optimal satisfaction.

Another factor that is led by the above is to determine the future demands for library development. Because, present problem will throw light upon the future prospect. Moreover, any investigation into the current problems will definitely forecast the possibilities of future requirements of the users which in turn will help the library planners to bring suitable reforms.

Users and the Five Laws of Library Science

Dr. S.R. Ranganathan in his philosophy of library science has accorded immense importance to the users. He has incorporated the concept of 'user' in a hidden manner in his five laws of library science. Because, these five laws centre round the user and the use of information. One can, therefore, describe the art of putting recorded knowledge or information to work/the use by the application of the following five laws of library service propounded by Dr. Ranganathan retaining the basic philosophy intact:

1. Information for use;
2. Every user his/her information;
3. Every information its user;
4. Save the time of information-user; and
5. An information system is a growing organism.

In the first law, he has categorically emphasised that information is to be utilised and exploited for its best use by the user. There is a clear indication of encouraging the use of information by the librarian for the user.

The second law, on the other hand, stressed the need of potential users for their specific information requirements at individual level. It refers to strategic aspects of the authority to develop proper organisation of information system and services so as to provide the required information to all its users.

It is the information specialist, as the third law says, to promote effective use of information as custodian, agent and interpreter for the potential users. It denotes the right information for the right users at a right point of time.

It is an accepted obligation on the part of the information organisation to develop proper and adequate mechanism so as to ensure maximum speed and effectiveness in providing right and appropriate information to its users just to save their time, which is the real motive of the fourth law.

The fifth law, however, says that an information system is a growing organism that inculcates the trio of information organisation—the specialist, the user, and the information proper—which is one of the most important constituents of the information system. The growing number of users provide pace to the growth of information to an extent beyond one's expectation.

It seems that Dr. Ranganathan's five laws of library science give adequate weightage to users because, they constitute as the most vital and primary component of the system for which, the whole information system is destined. Again these laws offer an excellent framework for undertaking conceptual studies on user and its associated concepts.

The 'use' and the 'user' concepts as reflected in the five laws, give much impetus and new dimensions to the problems of the library-user in particular. This force, therefore, has propelled the researchers in the field to know more about their users and to devise new methods and techniques for understanding them and implementing the strategic outcomes towards proper improvement of the existing conditions and developing new systems and techniques for their libraries best suited to their emerging needs.

Genesis and Development of User Studies

The capability of users to select and use of information independently is a problem of vital concern to the libraries and information centres. The review of user studies show a strong interest in analysing the information needs and channels of information-flow. Since the first quarter of the 20th century, library workers have developed curiosity over their users. While a library is primarily meant for the users, all its activities and operations centred to a library are directed towards user satisfaction. In order to achieve the optimal satisfaction of the users, the librarian has to keep a very close contact with its users knowing their reading interests, behaviour, information privations, and attitudes towards the library. These attempts can largely be considered as informal studies on users.

The libraries during the first quarter of the last century are believed to have traditionally used to study their users through the records kept, especially the circulation record. Sometimes, the librarian used to find the use of catalogues, reference service-related records and records concerning library use by various age groups for conducting user studies.

The second quarter of the last century witnessed a spectacular change in the structure, organisation and management of libraries, besides their rapid and extensive expansion. The most popular type of study undertaken during the said period was mainly on this type of study, almost everything related in anyway to the use of the library was researched (Tobin, 1974: p. 100) with new methodology of research called 'operation research', which was entered into the field of LIS. User studies gradually became an object of research using the methods of this operation research.

On the onset of second half of the last century, a vast number of studies were undertaken. The "Bibliography of Use-Surveys, 1950–1970" compiled by Atkins gives the evidence of nearly 687 studies for all types of libraries except for special libraries for which, 1,200 studies have been undertaken (Kawatra, 1992: p. 100). In academic libraries, there were over 100 such studies conducted (Ford, 1978). Wood in his studies "Factors Influencing Student Library Use: An Analysis of Studies" presents a useful analysis and summary of some of the major studies on library use during the period 1930-1964.

Krikelas (1983: p. 6) has also brought out a "Catalogue User Studies and Their Implications" that includes a chronology of catalogue use studies during 1930-1970.

The Centre of Research in User Study of the Sheffield University has brought out certain guidelines for the United Nations Educational, Scientific and Cultural Organisation (UNESCO) for study of information-user. *The Annual Review of Information Science and Technology* makes a review of user studies and has been publishing the reports of research work on such user studies at regular intervals. The Library Literature and LISA used to index the current work taken up on user studies. In addition to this, there are a number of studies on library users, which do not see the light of print. These unpublished studies furnish sufficient amount of information on growth and development of research on use, non-use and misuse of library material by the users.

If one tries to trace the development of user studies, it will be seen that the real growth of user studies was mostly activated by two international conferences, namely, (i) The Royal Society's Conference held in London in 1948, and (ii) the Washington Conference of 1958 (Devarajan, 1989: p. 5). Prior to these two conferences, an early user study in the field, however, was conducted in the late 1930s by the well-known scholars, Louis R. Watson which was an attempt to investigate the distribution and status of libraries in the United States (ibid.). A study entitled "Pilot Study on the Use of Scientific Literature by Scientists" conducted by Ralph R. Shaw is considered another milestone in the history of user studies.

During 1950s and 1960s, user studies were conducted on a very limited scale. The other user studies that drew attention of the contemporary scholars include: (i) a study carried out by Glock, Menzel, Glessnor and Sewers involving the interview of 77 sample scientists to discover their information needs and information gathering habits, (ii) study made by Voight (1959-60) to determine the approach of scientists to information, (iii) a comprehensive bibliography on user studies compiled by Davis and Bailey in 1964 containing 438 studies deserve special mention. Grawford also reported that by 1977, more than 1,000 important studies were conducted on user studies (Prasad, 1992: pp. 80-81).

The present trend of research in LIS however, lays adequate attention on the use of library material for the optimal satisfaction of its users for which they are intended. The trend of user studies further shows that the present rate of studies on the subject is increasing year after year (Devarajan, 1989 p. 6). Undoubtedly, the review of user studies shows a strange interest in analysing the information-flow among the users of various classes.

Classification of User Studies

User study is broadly a technique used to assess the pattern of using resources. While identifying the use pattern, the researcher can be able to examine and discover certain other factors associated with the use of resources. Since there is no fixed principles concerning taxonomical decisions of user studies, grouping of user studies varies from author to author. Menzel (Prasad, 1992: p. 77) has classified the user studies under three broad groups. They are:

1. Studies dealing with user behaviour;
2. Studies dealing with the information-use; and
3. Studies dealing with information-flow.

User-Behaviour or Behaviour Studies

User study is primarily a method of identifying the behavioural pattern of the users. In other words, user study is designed to reflect the information-seeking behaviour of the users in a given library system and environment. The interaction of the user is more a factor, which is verified and determined while identifying his attitudes towards the library resources.

Use of Literature on Information-Use Studies

The pattern of using literature by the users can be a form of user study. That can give a deep insight into the information handling and building a collection development for libraries as well as improving the user and the information intermediary interaction so as to provide the information services effectively. In other words, studies that are conducted to find out the use of any communication medium falls under the ambit of information-use studies.

Information Needs or Information-Flow Studies

The concept of information needs, which is confined to the studies of users, use and uses, forms one of the most extensive and amorphous areas of research in LIS today. Information needs under the ambit of user study is primarily designed to find out the pattern of library use, information systems, library materials and catalogue, and such other tools, information-seeking and gathering habits of various groups of users including the use of myriad information/sources.

R.G. Prasher (1991: p. 208), on the other hand, has classified the user studies under the four broad divisions, perhaps, taking the type of explanation provided in the studies into account. These four divisions are: (i) descriptive studies, (ii) analytical studies, (iii) survey-based studies, and (iv) user-based studies. All these studies, however, seem to have attempted the users as the focal point of their respective research.

Classification of Users

An information system is a heterogeneous phenomenon which consists of various user groups and sub-groups. A library user can be any person needing information from a system. A user can be distinguishable by the type of information he/she needs. The users of one type of library are essentially different from those of another type. Information-users, therefore, can be classified on the basis of their typology, occupation, the purposes for which they need information, their age, qualification, and professional position, etc. The total population of main user groups primarily fall under two basic groups. They are: (i) actual users, and (ii) potential users (Lazer, 1985: p. 50).

Actual users are those persons, who actually use information from an information system/library. The other group consists of persons, who do not make use of the services of an information system, but have the potential to become users. They are, therefore, known as potential users.

A library and information system is more concerned with the actual users compared to the latter category. In terms of the information needs, a user can be a student, teacher, scientist, engineer, journalist, technologist, researcher, physician, manager or a planner. Taking into consideration the duty and responsibility, nature of job they perform, the position they hold and needs and attitude they develop, the users of information may be classified into the following three categories (Atherton, 1977: p. 124):

1. Researchers in the basic science.
2. Practitioners and technicians engaged in development.
3. Managers, planners and decision-makers.

The exhaustiveness of this grouping has left some other core users of information. To define broadly, the users of information in accordance with classification principles, they can either be living and non-living entities. Under living users, they are individuals or group of individuals. And under non-living entity, they are organisations, institutions and other corporate bodies, who primarily deal with information for various developmental and operational activities.

However, in either case, an information manager or the librarian, in order to provide meaningful and effective information service, should ascertain the exact information requirements of his library-users. In fact, he should reply to himself as to who are his users. What are their needs? How do they approach to information? How do they behave while using information? Answers to these questions are imminent on the part of the librarian so as to justify its existence.

Methods and Techniques Used in User Studies

User study is the job of an information researcher designed to assess the psychological and social attributes of the user. Readers' preferences, choices, attitudes, and interests are determined on the basis of information they require. A thorough and deep study is usually made to measure their pattern of information behaviour so as to influence and design an information system. This user study can be undertaken by a number of methods and techniques.

In user study, the unit of analysis is typically the individual person, but there can be a group or an entity. In other words, it is called sampling the population. Several methods are now used to try and achieve the goal of sampling, which is to avail the set of representative of the population being studied.

Survey method used in social science research seems to be the most widely accepted research techniques. Here, the approach is that a sample of individuals having worked in the specific field or experiences are requested to provide certain information. The response obtained there from them constitutes the data upon which the research hypotheses are examined. This method is called survey method. Survey technique cover any or all the facts of a library or information system including myriad characteristics of users themselves. The following criteria can be considered while undertaking a survey on users.

In order to evaluate the decision-making process and assessing the effectiveness of the library system, it is essential to determine the purpose fulfilling library and information system and level of success of a variety of programmes and services, so as to assist in designing, continuing, modifying the existing programmes and services, to establish priorities among programmes and services and to solve specific problems in order to overcome deficiencies, if any, found in the existing system.

To establish user interaction with the system, it is imperative to determine the level of user satisfaction and attitudes, to identify users' successes and failures, to determine the patterns and levels of use, to ascertain the potential and actual users, and along with their information privations and subject preferences.

User characteristics play a vital role in the survey in which the factors like user interests, lifestyles, information-flow and literature-use habits, information sources they seek and trends and needs, etc., matter more crucial.

Although a number of methods are followed in user survey, three major methods seem to be popularly used to elicit information from respondents. They are: (i) personal interview, (ii) the questionnaires, and (iii) the telephone survey (Nachmias and Nachmias, 1991: p. 181). There are other methods like observation, analysis of library records, citation analysis, etc., which are also being applied by some scholars taking the typical environment of individual library into account.

Interview is a face-to-face interpersonal role situation, in which the interviewer asks respondents questions designed to obtain answers pertinent to the research hypothesis. The questions, their wording and sequence define the extent to which the interview is structured. The structured interview involves the use of a set of predetermined questions and of highly standardised techniques of recording. Against this, the unstructured interview appears to be the central technique of collecting information research studies. Interview of users, most of the time, reveals data on user and non-user attitudes and perceptions about library use. The response received therefrom gives the greatest amount of probing and answer-seeking.

Another method of survey of users is telephone interview. It is characterised as a semi-personal method of collecting information. This method has gained general acceptance over the last few years as a substitute for personal interviewing. It is convenient and produces a significant cost-saving and higher response.

Questionnaire method is normally regarded as an impersonal survey method. In this process, a clearly and specifically defined group of users are asked to answer a number of identical questions. These individuals are administered with a questionnaire either by local distribution or through mail with an onus to fill out on their own. This method seems to be the most suitable and convenient due to its lower cost, greater autonomy and accessibility. A questionnaire is the most common accepted device used in measuring library-use and users' attitudes towards library resources. This technique gives detail information about users' habit, perception on the functioning of the library and opinion on improving the standard of existing library services.

Observation is regarded as the basic, most primitive and widely accepted modern method of scientific research. Scientific research begins with observation and ends in observation. It includes the most casual, uncontrolled experience and practical experimentation. User study in the library environments can be undertaken in observing the phenomena primarily associated with the library-use. By observation, information concerning to different behaviour patterns of the users can be collected in the library without putting any obvious burden on the part of the users. Most of the user studies conducted through observation method in the libraries are confined to the use of card catalogues, circulation of library material, type of reference queries they put and the extent of their independent approach to library resources.

Guha (Devarajan, 1989: pp. 7-9), however, has grouped the existing techniques for user studies under three main heads which include:

1. general or conventional methods,
2. indirect methods, and
3. special and unconventional methods.

General or Conventional Methods

Under this category, methods such as survey methods like questionnaire, interview, diary, observation by self, and operation research are most popular. Of these, questionnaire and interview methods are found to have been used extensively by the LIS researchers engaged in user studies.

Indirect Methods

This method, as the name implies, helps to collect data in an indirect way, i.e., without coming in contact with the users directly. This method is primarily associated with the citation analysis and analysis of library-related records. On the basis of the material used by the library clienteles, the researcher can ascertain the users' requirements indirectly. Some of the important records that need to be examined include circulation statistics, inter-library loan records, personal indexes used by the researchers, service demand slips of the reference section, users' profile, etc., can be used. Analysis of the foregoing records, according to Devarajan (ibid.), provides only a partial view of user needs or requirements.

Quite a good number of scholars in the field of user studies, seem to have used citation analysis as an alternative and most popular technique for user studies. Citation or references provided by authors in their documents become the basis of citation analysis. The implicit assumption is that the cited documents, which are used by the authors become an index to the nature of materials required by the users. According to Devarajan (ibid.) though citation analysis, compared to other methods, is mostly viewed as unbiased, gives rise to a number of perils. These include:

1. citation analysis gives only a partial idea about the use of materials as secondary and tertiary sources, formal and informal sources, etc., which in fact, are not usually cited by the authors;
2. the possibility of their citing unused material; and
3. the possibility of self-citation by certain authors.

Special and Unconventional Methods

This method includes computer feedback, which makes use of records obtained as by-products of a computer search with the emergence of modern technologies, extensive use of computers in libraries and information centres easily brings this technique into an effective one in ascertaining the requirements of the users. By this method, the researcher tries to know the way in which the scientists work, the formal and informal channels of communication they use, etc., so as to make his studies meaningful and effective.

However, Paisley and Parker (Sarcevic, 1970: p. 88) described the methodology required for gathering information about information-use pattern in a different fashion. According to them, such methods can be grouped mainly under three broad categories, namely:

1. by asking people about it;
2. by observing its occurrence; and
3. by examining its artifacts.

These methods can be used either individually or in a combination of two or more methods depending upon the nature and scope of the problem and the number of users to be studied (Maheswarappa and Hiremath, 1995: p. 293). Since each method or technique has its own merits and limitations, the scholars should be careful in choosing a method suitable to his own population, environment in order to arrive at just findings.

Trends in User Studies

Researchers in the LIS, as the time marches, have laid much emphasis on user studies, particularly in the field of LIS research. As a result, the research literature in the field of LIS, particularly during the last decade, witnessed a spectacular growth in all its ramifications. During the 1930s, when early researches on user studies were undertaken, the scope then was mostly limited to inside the library. But taking into consideration the variety of users in multidisciplinary field, such studies were undertaken concerning to the problems of the users beyond the library premises. The same phenomenon can be exemplified through an illustration in which, two such studies, i.e., one concerning to inside the library or other outside the library of the University of Colorado were undertaken. The study concerning outside the library, i.e, student union is a better represented study of library-use compared to the study made within the library premises.

Library being the centre of information for both science and social science research, researchers have stressed the need for developing an effective communication setting so as to make a sound system for free flow of information. To practise the same, communication, as a scientific method of dissemination, was adopted to provide a comprehensive description of all facts of the subjects concerned. Also furnish the expanded form APA Project of Scientific Information Exchange in Psychology, for instance, applied several methods and techniques to bring out a comprehensive picture of the free flow of information in psychology and of the characteristics of all major media used to acquire and disseminate information in the concerned field. This study was more concerned with the participants, who were seeking specific information through their attendance, their success in obtaining it, and the nature of information they sought.

Another well-known trend is the recognition of the social role of the scientific communication as reflected in the studies of invisible college. Since the information generators are also among the principal users, the system continuously feedsback on itself. With the adoption of system approach to the study of scientific communications, inter-relations and interdependence of various methods of communication system too have received increased attention.

N.G. Satish (1994: pp. 26-27) in his work 'Attitude Towards Information' mentions one definite trend that is, however, discerned towards comprehensive description of all facts of scientific communication in particular disciplines. The major trend in the communication research, which he maintains include growing awareness of social characters and social organisation of scientific communication as reflected in the studies made by Derek J. De S. Price and Donald De B. Beaver (1966: pp. 1011–18) on invisible college; and defining the role of scientific meeting and enhancing its effectiveness as a means of information exchange.

Early models of user studies are more related to the document-seeking and library-use. Researchers used to confine their work on the practical aspects of library usage by the users. The centre of their attention was more of the library than that of the user. All the early models of user studies were primarily concerned with document-seeking or library use than with the characteristics of behaviour, which might usefully discriminate among information-users and provide guidance to service planning. On the other hand, Wilson (1981: pp. 3-15) also recognises the necessity of identifying the ends served by the information-seeking behaviour within the wider contact of users' totality of experiences or users' life-world centred upon the individual as an information-user. He feels much of the user studies in the past have suffered from a concentration as the means by which people discover information, analysed in terms of how the users ought to have been seeking information.

However, during the later period, there was a shift in the focus. The behaviour of the users and the coverage received utmost attention in most of the studies. Information-user, as an organisational user, influenced the whole spectrum of information environment and was taken as a model of study. "Information Requirement of Social Scientists (INFROSS)", a study taken at Bath University (Line et al., 1971) can be accepted as a remarkable example in the field of user studies. This study, in fact, gave a new direction to the problem associated with the user study especially in social sciences having identified the deep understanding of the behavioural pattern of the social science-users.

Another study conducted at the Bath University in 1973 on "Design of Information Systems for Social Science Project", a milestone in analysis of the requests made to the National Children's Bureau Questions and Answers Service, is a user evaluation of an information service in social welfare (Satish, 1994: p. 34). This study, in fact, had shown that while 65 per cent of the enquiries were for information in a great variety of particular subjects, less than 35 per cent of users, on the other hand, asked for references, various research findings and statistics.

A three-phased research project on "Information Needs and Information Services in Local Authority Social Science Department (INISS)" undertaken in 1975 to experiment the multifaceted problems of the users aptly concludes that specialisation of information services according to the scheduled work roles where common needs can be discerned is desirable and information services should be integrated in the organisations communication pattern (Wilson and Stretfield, 1979: pp. 120-30).

The foregoing studies have, therefore, established the fact that a more comprehensive description of all facts of scientific communication in a given discipline becomes the pre-requisite for every information system. The scholars in present trend should, therefore, agree that user studies should primarily be concerned with the document-seeking approach of the library-users rather than their behaviour.

User Studies in India

An in-depth review of literature on the subject clearly shows that a considerable number of user studies have been conducted concerning the use of individual libraries by the various scientists and the general public alike. The outcome of few such studies which have set examples for the future scholars and the LIS professionals, testing the gravity of the individual library environment, provided a sufficient scope for the library concerned to revamp the whole system and to rebuild the library collection so as to make it more purposive, need-based and meaningful for those it is intended.

Carl M. White's study on University of Delhi Library in 1965 was the first of its kind in India (ibid.), which gave a detailed account of the library development in regards to its services. No definite standard for use in developing a university library programme exists. Among other things, the quality aspects of the library development rather than 'users' approach' seem to have been predetermined in his recommendations.

Krishan Kumar's study (1973) on the Use of Sapru House Library serving social science teachers and scholars provides sufficient clue concerning the average number days and hours the library is put to use, along with the priority of information sources being explored, thereby giving a scope for the library administrator to reorient the library system suitable to the requirements of social scientists.

Dhanyi conducted a survey of 100 readers at Rajasthan University Library in 1974, which revealed that readers demonstrated their interest more in using the library at college level with an optimal approach to library catalogue and handling reference books. The study stressed the need for user education for the new entrants of the college library.

The other such studies that deserve mention include the study made by Karuna Shah (1975) on the quantum of library use and pressure of demand from various categories of users, the study of Karki (1982) on "Analysis of Industrial Information Service in India" and Rajgopalan and Rajan's (1985) on user studies on users of LIS periodicals are some of the notable works in the field.

The seminar on "User Studies and User Education" held in Osmania University on 1985 also stressed the need for conducting user studies in Indian university libraries. The libraries have to conduct user studies, so that they can prepare an acquisition policy which can help in acquiring appropriate information best suited to their clientele.

The work on user studies, particularly in India, very often followed the findings of the studies taking place in United

Kingdom and USA, which are primarily based on theoretical and review type without providing adequate data on observation. In addition to these, several such lesser studies have also been conducted at Master and M. Phil level dissertations of library schools in the country, but are relatively inaccessible as most of them remained unpublished.

User Studies on Journalists

Journalists occupy a very distinct place in the communication system of a country, as because they shape ideas, events, opinions and problems in terms of news that tremendously influence the society. Journalists significantly dominate a whole print media of a nation, which apparently reflects their social position, profession and missionary objectives in making the nation more informative. Since public opinion is more crucial and viable force than the contribution of the journalists, truthful and unbiased news-reporting are highly essential to the successful working of any democratic system (UNESCO, 1981: p. 233).

Journalists of the developing countries in particular, very often make the right to seek information imperative without any hindrance, so as to communicate the same more effectively. Hence, journalists' access to, and need for information appears to be of great significant for research scholars of LIS.

It is the distinct obligation of a librarian or information scientist, among other things, to know the user community better by assessing their information needs and determining their information-seeking behaviour. In performing such a difficult task, the librarian has to understand the users and to acquaint himself with their myriad information requirements, so as to ascertain the impact of the library on the lifestyle of the users, who can contribute substantially to social, political and economical environment of the nation.

Studying users and use of resources will ultimately pave the way for the librarian to design an effective information system tailored to the needs of the target audience. Hence, users study is one of the crucial weapons, through which the information requirements of the journalists can be better addressed and the significant results thereof can be analysed to find out the most suitable methods of service/delivery which can help to develop an appropriate information system for them in India. Since no such comprehensive study has yet been undertaken concerning journalists as potential users of the libraries, the present study becomes imminent.

3

Information

At the edge of 20th century, the society entered into a period popularly called as 'information age'. All the human activities are directed towards information-producing and information-consuming practices. In the USA, more than 46 per cent of Gross National Product (GNP) and 53 per cent of labour income is related to knowledge, communication and information (Hanna, 1991: p. 39). In Organisation for Economic Cooperation and Development (OECD) countries, the information sector alone accounts for one-third to one-half of Gross Domestic Product (GDP) and of employment. According to Wellenius, by the year 2000, this sector was expected to grow to 60 per cent of the European community GDP (Zijp, 1994: p. 3). Parallel to this phenomenon, similar situation is being witnessed in other developing countries with most of their activities being related to information.

With the march of time, information has become the central focus of human living. The new dimensions and spheres of telecommunication, television, telematics, computer related information retrieval techniques along with digital technologies, publishing firms, radio, satellite communication, etc., are at crossroads. The people engaged on other sectors like agriculture, industry, research and development, bureaucracy, journalism and entertainment are running after information of one kind or other. Their jobs are based on information ideas and information technology. They used to perform the tasks, which normally involve collecting, processing, storing, disseminating, and using information in several forms for different purposes. These activities that consider information as the central theme materially affect individuals, organisations, societies, economies, and the whole humanity as well, bringing about a new socio-economic value to the present society. In other words, this emerging phenomenon is rooted in the concept 'information'.

'Information' in one form or other has consistently been a significant element in the development of human society and that it has shaped over a long period of time, the way in which one thinks and acts (Stevans, 1986: p. 2). The essence of information is a critical factor not only for the countries, but also for the individuals besides its multiplier effect on the efficiency and effectiveness of an entity for which it is utilised. As information is used by all human beings more or less to take decisions in their routine lives and to get the positive result out of it, the need for right information at the right time is highly crucial. This being the sole aim of any service system, the importance of information in every sector of human activity is a matter of great concern not only to librarians, but also to the policy makers, planners, administrators, scientists and researchers alike.

The history of information can be dated back to the early civilisation when the development of writing in papyrus and clay tablets was started and knowledge-organisation with the generation of ideas related to printing was christened. The development of writing and invention of printing is an important component of the history of information. Einstein has examined the question of the kinds of changes in communication and learning brought about by printing and its impact on the intellectual and political revolutions of early modern times. However, Stevans, for the sake of convenience, divides the entire study of history of information under three broad periods, namely, pre-history, the age of writing, and the printing. Less is known about the real history of information. Hence, it needs a detailed study.

If human society is said to be really marching towards development and progress, it is only due to information. Its value as a vital resource for socio-economic changes has never been challenged. If one finds the human history, one can witness tremendous changes in the process of social evolution with three different stages in which the role of information is the mainstay. In the agrarian society, the bit of information put to the minds of the farmers brought out radical changes in the pattern of agrarian process, products and methods of farming so that, the emerging changes in the livelihood of the people could be felt. The second stage is that of an industrial society, where information is primarily considered to be the main spirit behind the growth and development of an industrial world. In the words of noted futurist, Alvin Toffler (1970: p. 176) the post-industrial society is information society in which the striking changes are dramatically arrived directly affecting people and organisations in their workplace, at home, and their behavioural patterns.

The present era of information age is christened with the advent of electronics, telecommunication, telematics, computer and other technological advancements—all related to procuring, processing, preserving, disseminating, and using of information. The large-scale and uncontrolled deluge of publications has made the society overwhelmed with information. With the changing pace of modern life, the concept of information got adequate momentum. The diffusion and dispersion of information has also made people awake to their potential requirements. Just as modern money penetrated the whole world within less than a century underwent sea-changes in people's lives and aspirations, thereby assuming that 'information' now penetrates everywhere (Drucker, 1993: p. 328). Information, therefore, moves everywhere and as such its effects are pervasive. Information-man and information-based organisations are doing tremendous jobs for the development of the society. Every effort is being made to create an information-rich environment.

The essence of information and its impact on society has been tremendously realised in all walks of life, as it is very much crucial to the social and economic activities that comprise the development process. Information is primarily considered an agent of social change. In every aspect of the development process, be it education, research, business, etc., information has far-reaching implications and consequences. It has also created new possibilities to attack vexing problems of poverty, inequality and environmental degradation with the potential to achieve unprecedented gains on economic and human development fronts (Talero and Gaudette, 1996: p. 11).

Recognising such a social transformation that information has brought about in magnifying, accelerating, reorganising and reshaping the society, the concept of global electronic village through internet has now rendered information sharing activities much faster than ever before. And, it is information that has brought about such a huge and worldwide concentration that generates new thoughts to study more on its nature, type, uses, needs and seeking behaviour which ultimately inflicts information-flow to understand and create suitable environments.

Information: Meaning and Definitions

Meaning

Information appears to be an ambiguous term, a term that is fluid and has several denotations. Because, it has connotative differences with several disciplines that use the concept 'information' in their concerned area of studies differently. Information may indicate different concepts both, between different disciplines such as philosophy, cybernetics, biology, communication theory, semiotics, and within disciplines including that of information science itself. The following representation shows how the term, 'information' is understood in different disciplinary approaches.

Disciplines		*Implications of Information*
Biological Sciences	:	Processing in living beings
Computer Science	:	Processing, storing and retrieving in mechanised form

Electrical Engineering	:	Transmission
Electronics	:	Communication
Philosophy	:	Epistemological study
Physical Sciences	:	As an abstraction and analogous of element, structure of communication
Psychology	:	Cognitive processing
LIS	:	Resource use, systems and services
Linguistic Areas	:	Expressing, conducting and communicating
Social Sciences	:	Resource and commodity
Journalism and Mass Communication	:	Reporting, conveying message to a large number of people

The above representation clearly demonstrates that the concept 'information' is being widely viewed as a subject of study for several disciplines and that they have their respective meanings and implications as concerned to their respective scope of activities.

The impact of information is, however, so diverse that the term 'information' is very often confused and understood in its relation to certain other associated concepts such as data, fact, observation, intelligence, skill, knowledge, experience, wisdom, etc. Although, these terms have their own etymological and implicational differences with information, the meaning and operational uses are more understood in information terms due to strong ties of interrelationship among them.

However, three terms, data, information and knowledge appear to be more synonymous, in spite of their differences in meanings. By a simple explanation, their meaning can be well differentiated.

'Data' are symbolic surrogates that represent people, objects, events and concepts in terms of words, numbers, symbols, etc. For example, scientific data in laboratory experiments, social data on population, price index, trade statistics, etc.

'Information' is an aggregate of facts and processed data which is communicated in a meaningful term. Examples: results of laboratory investigation, stock-exchange information, news of national and international events, etc.

On the other hand, knowledge is consolidated and structured information in concrete form or a phenomenon of mind.

However, these terms are so inextricably interwoven that in common parlance they seem to be synonymous. But it is necessary to comprehend the usage of these words for understanding varied professional purposes.

Definitions

The term 'information' is not confined to a single subject or discipline. This has led to the problems encountered in bringing the term into a specific confine with a common denominator. This has reflected in the continuous effort to develop generalised definitions for the concepts 'information' and 'information science', which until now are partially successful (Wellisch, 1972: p. 173).

Wellisch (ibid.) found some 39 definitions of information and information science, all of them not related to each other (Manda, 1991: p. 18). Most of these descriptions are partially valid only in a limited range of applications. Most of the authors are of the opinion that the term 'information' is used with different connotations and a single precise definition encompassing all its aspects in principle cannot be formulated.

Farradane (ibid.) defines 'information' as any physical form of representation or surrogate of knowledge or of a particular thought used for communication (ibid.).

In *Webster's Third International Dictionary*, the term, 'information' is defined as "the communication or reception of knowledge or intelligence, something obtained or received through informing, the process by which the form of all object of knowledge is impressed upon the apprehending mind so as to bring about the status of knowing" (Webster, 1978: p. 1160).

According to Shera, information is a fact. It is the stimulus, which one perceives through senses. This information may be a single isolated fact or it may be a whole cluster of facts; but it is still a unit of thought. It can have any dimension. It is that intellectual entity which one receives, the building block of knowledge (Babu, 1994: p. 22).

According to Schramm 'information' is the stuff of communication and that communication is the ability to process information and share it with others" (Dervin et al., 1982: p. 419).

Kent (1970: p. 16) states that information is the feedstock for knowledge. In an ideal world of unimpeded flow of information into knowledge, there would be an advantage to be gained by any individual or group compared with another by possession of information.

Wersig and Neveling (1975: pp. 127-40) however, in their study of "the phenomena of interest to information science" consider information much more comprehensively adopting six basic approaches, namely, the structural, the knowledge, the message, the meaning, the effect, and the process approach. The summary of these approaches is that information is a social process and can be understood if it is defined in relation to needs either as reduction to uncertainty caused by a communication data or as data used for reducing uncertainty.

The definition as given by Brookes, however, shows a different picture. He says that 'knowledge' is summation of many bits of information, which have been organised into some sort of coherent entity that can be represented by a simple equation. When information D1 is added to the existing body of knowledge K(S), it results in modified knowledge K(S + DS). This can be represented as: K(S) + D1 = K(S+DS) (1981: pp. 3-12).

'Information' as defined in *Oxford English Dictionary* gives rise to two propositions. They are:

1. Communication of instructive knowledge or news of some fact or occurrence, and

2. Knowledge-communication concerning some particular fact, subject or event.

Buckland (1995: p. 351), on the other hand, has segregated three different aspects of information. In his analysis, he considers (i) information as process; (ii) information as knowledge; and (iii) information as thing.

According to Davis and Olson (1985: p. 200) "'information' is data that has been processed into a form that is meaningful to the recipient and is of real or perceived value in current or prospective actions or decisions".

Over the years, a variety of more specific definitions of information have been found, ranging from the idea that information consists of assertions as to the state of affairs at a given news (Berlo, 1977: p. 33) to the idea that information is defined in terms of its potential for reducing cognitive uncertainty (Atkins, 1973: p. 205).

However, in the context of user studies research, the term 'information' is defined as a physical entity or phenomena, the channel of communication through which messages are transferred or the factual data are empirically determined and presented in a document or transmitted orally (Wilson, 1981: p. 3).

Although there are variations among these definitions, virtually all are based on a single theoretical formulation developed by Shannon and Weaver (1949).

Thus, taking together all these definitions, it can be summed up that 'information' is the intellectual property in one form or other that is conveyed or utilised to generate enriched and meaningful messages for creation of knowledge.

Information has, therefore, become so pervasive and widespread, both in its contents and dimensions that there can be no single definition, as there can be no single set of characteristics for the classification and grouping of it. Several attributes can be interwoven to the idea of information, such as, transfer process, properties, contextual subjects and uses. If one goes to interpret information differently, it would be obvious that several disciplines have information as their significant part of study and research. But a subject like LIS appears to have concentrated more on the 'concept of information' than any other discipline.

Information is primarily a basic necessity for the human being which is put to use to generate good or bad results. Its value can be realised on its use, the information provider or user, and the way they utilise information in their desired perspective ways. As it is evident that information reduces uncertainty, Prasher (1987: p. 96) argues that the degree of uncertainty varies from one person to other depending upon the time and place. Information generates value through the decision situation it creates and the decision it informs. By developing a relationship between information life cycle and decision-making, Manson, Manson and Culnan (1995: p. 51) have collectively determined five core components of information value-adding chain.

Beginning from the source, the data is desired in the second place, which then in the third stage, is given proper interpretation applying assumptions and perspective to the data. The fourth component, on the other hand, is the evaluation of inference drawn with regard to values that lead to action in the final stage. Information value-adding chain can be, therefore, worth noting with respect to two basic features. First, information is developed through several qualitatively different levels and the second being that points of articulation between different parties often characterise the flow of information from source to action. In decision-making, the nature and amount of information changes the behaviour of the individual recipients.

Characteristics of Information

Information is a resource of immense socio-economic value. Its use in social restructuring and nation-building is vital as it affects every aspect of development. The centrality to the concept of 'information' is its communication and use. The work of any developmental user, i.e., scientists, technologists, teachers, researchers, managers, etc., necessitates effective communication, on which one's complete result and achievement depends. The question of communication and use of information are based upon its nature, characteristics and properties. The following description illustrates the importance of the attributes of information in a broader perspective.

Paisley and Hardy (1980: p. 26) have suggested some of the factors—the factors that are related to the use of services of information by individuals. Their contention is that the value of information can be defined in terms of attributes related to the settings in which information is used. These attributes include relevance, timeliness, comprehensiveness, authoritativeness, specificability, locatability, acquirability and usability. The value of a piece of information with respect to the above attributes may vary in respect to the undermentioned factors as suggested by Paisley:

1. the way in which the information is used including its use in learning, decision-making, problem-solving, calculation, and verification;
2. characteristics of the individual seeking information including their preferences for cognitive complexity or simplicity, the paradigm with which they structure a field and the extent to which they differentiate, and the various levels of information;
3. social and organisational factors including characteristics of the work-team, work organisation, and professional disciplinary groups to which an individual belongs; and
4. task requirements including, whether the problems encountered in a given task are recurring or episodic.

Cleveland, however, has taken a different view, in identifying the distinguishing characteristics of information. According to him, information is human, expandable, compressible, substitutable, transportable, diffusive and shareable. These attributes make the concept 'information' a unique resource and its use that creates an epoch in the modern information environment (Manson, 1995: p. 42).

Considering information as human, it is propounded that information exists in the human mind. Information is abstract and psychological in nature as it lives in the human being because, it is primarily a mind-based entity. The cognitive structure of human brain generates and processes information. Therefore, information is the result of mental activity of mind that observes, imagines, remembers, analyses, compares, relates, organises, intuits and integrates.

Information can also be expanded in its use. The attribute, 'expandability' means that any item of information is used or produced, creates new information and such its scope and limit get expanded.

Information is compressible. Information contained in complex system and services are compiled, integrated, summarised, indexed, abstracted, thereby, its very communication is compressed. The librarians and information scientists use several methods in condensing the information for better understanding of the users.

Information can be substituted for any material for which it is used. Substitutability is one of the major sources of information's power and can be used to improve human condition(s) (Manson, 1995: p. 44).

It is a well-known and acknowledged fact that information is transportable. From the early times, several methods were undertaken to transfer message from one place to another. Using modern technology, it has become very easy and cheap to transmit messages. All the technologies are directed towards achieving sophisticated and speedy transmission of information from the point of generation to the point of use across the world. Major changes have been witnessed in both speed and volume of the movement of information, particularly owing to technological revolutions and Internet. The basic phenomenon of this transportability is to ensure the use and sharing of information in a global sphere.

Information is more concerned with knowledge diffusion. Because, it has got to be diffused for various developmental purposes. This process of diffusion and dissemination adds value to primary information.

The shareable feature of information is the most significant factor in regards to its use. Adding to the concept of information, new dimension of sharing has been evolved, giving subsequent development to networking among information centres and providers. Few such well-known networks are OCLC, UTLAS, WLN, RLIN and many others.

Properties of Information

An examination of information and its components gives rise to the need for assessing its inherent properties for which its essence and existence appears to be prominent in human use. Burt Nanun (1981: p. 56) found that information has unique properties in terms of the following attributes:

1. Information is extremely heterogeneous;
2. It is of least value, unless otherwise interpreted or used in specific contexts;
3. Demand for information depends upon variables like age, perishability, convenience, reliability, source, cost, quality, quantity, and availability;
4. Information appears to be the central focus in management and functioning of an organisation meant for production; and
5. Copyright, intellectual property right and patent laws are to be provided for safeguarding the values of information products.

However, the properties of information can be analysed on the basis of its utility in specific fields or areas. In general connotation, the concept of information has certain universal properties applicable to all. Thus, information in common parlance is not consumable in use, shared by many without any loss, and a democratic resource that can be used by everybody, of course, barring few exceptions to official secrecy now in vogue in few countries. Information is, therefore, continuous, dynamic and ever-growing without any end to it.

In scientific and technical parlance, information has certain unique properties. In physical and biological sciences, information is universal in its content and it can be available to all in an organised communication system. The quality of information is enhanced with the review of peer groups. Information in these areas are prone to obsolescence due to fast-growing/changing phenomenon associated with it. The present exponential growth of scientific literature has made information inaccessible and unavailable to certain extent.

In present technological environment, information has got free as well as restricted flow in the sense of time and geographical barriers that has made its value more sought for.

Taxonomy of Information

The use of information in society is so complex and myriad in nature that there cannot be a single category of information. Even if there is certain category, it is, however, difficult to differentiate without any basis. In fact, information can be categorised using different characteristics that depend upon the purpose of such grouping.

According to Koblitz (1969), 'information' can be of three kinds:

1. Semantic information (as a message),
2. Semantic information (as a process), and
3. Documental information.

While, semantic information as a message is used for transmission of knowledge, the same as a process is used to store and disseminate on a permanent basis. On the other hand, documental information having the characteristics of analytical and synthetic nature is full of facts, statistics or statements supported by evidences.

Bhattacharya (1978: pp. 18-20) has, however, categorised information under two broad groups:

1. Discursive information, and
2. Non-discursive information.

Discursive information is the message conveyed by a systematised body of ideas or its accepted or acceptable substitutes, having one or more of the following attributes relating to its treatment of explosion:

1. Ranging over a wide field;
2. Proceeding logically or coherently from topic to topic; and
3. Reasoning from premises to conclusion or proceeding from particular to general utilising analytical reasoning or proceeding from logical abstraction to logical interaction.

Non-discursive information, on the other hand, is a unit of facts conveyed by a systematised body or its accepted or acceptable substitutes. Further, non-discursive information, on the other hand, is sub-divided into two types:

1. Qualitative; and
2. Quantitative.

According to Badwen (1986: p. 210), however, information can be of four types (1986: p. 210). These are:

1. Interdisciplinary information;
2. Peripheral information;
3. Speculative information; and
4. Exceptions and inconsistencies.

This taxonomically division of information is more creative in nature and in that it provides adequate sustenance for developing idea(s) generated in human mind.

Another classical categorisation of information has been provided by Shera (1972: p. 175). He has formulated such a categorisation of information, which is primarily based on the process of generation. Thus, information, according to him, can be studied under six broad groups:

1. Conceptual information;
2. Empirical information;
3. Procedural information;
4. Stimulatory information;
5. Policy information; and
6. Directory information.

Types of information have been judged by Christie (1991: p. 39) from different angles taking into account the following four broad dimensions: (i) relating to behaviour; (ii) organisational penetration; (iii) item content; and (iv) technological fit.

From behavioural patterns, however, information can be of only two types. They are: (a) general, which is more of relating to purpose, and (b) specific that relates to the psychological mechanism involved. On the basis of organisational penetration, three fundamental types of information can identified. These are:

1. Material information;
2. System information; and
3. Product information.

An organisation requires the above three types of information to produce informative materials, viz., document either in printed or non-printed form. Here, it can be ascribed that the types of information distinguished above are primarily concerned with the organisational effectiveness for production and consumption of documents.

In respect to item content, information can be divided into two types:

1. Data information, and
2. Programme information.

While data information refers to statistical numbers, symbols, etc., that are used in specific purposes, programme information, on the other hand, is manipulated to show how former is utilised.

The fourth key type under this dimensions, i.e., technological fit, is less significant due to the introduction of electronic system that handles a wider spectrum of information.

Despite the above categorisation of information formulated by several authors, a broad grouping of information has been done on the basis of a set of common characteristics. The modified model of information transfer of Shanan and Weaver is the base of such characteristics that groups information depending upon the purpose of its use. These characteristics can be source, channel, media, recipient and information needs.

Under this type of grouping, information can be of the following types [Indira Gandhi National Open University (IGNOU) materials, 1996].

Information Grouping

Sources	*Channel*	*Media*
1. Signals	1. Literature (Primary, Secondary and Tertiary)	1. Oral
2. Text	2. Information	2. Recorded
3. Graphics	3. Distribution agencies	

Recipient	*Information Needs*	
	By Standard	*By Type*
1. Individuals	1. Popular	1. know-why
2. Groups	2. Scientific	2. know-how
3. Organisations	3. Technical	3. show-how
4. Institutions		

The study on taxonomical division of information, therefore, reveals that categorisation of information varies from entities to environments. In a particular situation, information has specific categories which are quite irrelevant to a different setting. For example, information concerning a health service environment has the followings categories:

1. Scientific, clinical and health service information;
2. Patient-generated clinical information;
3. Corporate activity management information; and
4. Information for patients, carriers and the general public.

In journalism and mass communication, information can be categorised into two types: (i) current information, and (ii) retrospective information.

While current information is more used to design a news item as the recent happening or events, retrospective information, on the other hand, is said to be helpful in fabricating a feature article to substantiate the facts.

These types of information, however, are exclusively designed to affect a definite environment for which its categorisation is meaningful.

Principles and Qualities of Information

The basic concepts and ideas as propounded by Ranganathan in his five laws are the fundamental tenets of library science. These laws show a significant move towards establishing a dynamic theory by which the very fabric of the discipline is based upon. Information science is the 'brainchild' of librarianship and the laws generated for the Library Science to be functional can be considered synonymous with information science.

In a corollary to the five laws of Library Science, Bhattacharya (Khanna, 1985: p. 73), however, has derived the five basic principles of information. These are:

1. Information is for use.
2. Every information-user his/her information.
3. Every piece of information, its user.
4. Save the time of information-user.
5. The universe of information is ever growing.

It is very often remarked that information is a valuable resource having certain qualities for its effective use. Rojas (Devarajan, 1989: p. 2) has identified some of the important qualities of information. These are:

1. accessibility,
2. comprehensiveness,
3. precision,
4. compatibility,
5. timeliness,
6. clarity,
7. flexibility,
8. verifiability,
9. free of bias, and
10. quantifiable.

These aforesaid qualities of information appear to be the essential conditions by which the use of information in an effective way can be ensured.

But, William (1965) has determined six other parameters of information that are considered as equivalent to qualities. These can be discussed as under:

1. Quality of information can be measured by the quantity of information contents in pages, words, characters, bits, etc.;
2. Quality corresponds to the contents and meaning;
3. Structure and organisation of information and its logical relationship between statements and elements;
4. Ideas expressed in the documents using language, symbols, codes and syntax;
5. Completeness, accuracy, relevance and timeliness of information; and
6. Value obtained from information in the time span.

In any system or services dealing with information dissemination for its users, there needs be an approach of agreement for greater reliability and accuracy of information provided. Information must conform to reality, so as its trustworthiness can be ensured. If up-to-date information cannot be provided, the value of its use will be deemed to lose its credibility. The information intermediary while analysing and disseminating information must ensure the attributes of quality which can satisfy the recipients in a manner that conform to their information privations. That is why, the system should generate the idea of quality in respect to reliability, accuracy, reality, nascency completeness, certainty and intelligibility. In an effort to ensure quality of information, librarians used to interpret, classify, catalogue, store, analyse and update in a manner that permits in their scope. However, the application of information technology is designed to ensure dissemination of error-free clientele-friendly and qualitative information, detecting bias and improving the quality beyond human imagination.

Information Resources

It is the inherent attitude of man to preserve his thoughts and ideas for the future generations. From earliest times to the present day, people have kept their ideas, thoughts, emotional feelings in written/recorded form through a variety of materials: bone, clay, metal, wax, wood, papyrus, leather, parchment, paper, film, plastic, and magnetic tape and finally in optical disc. Behind their attempt to preserve these materials for posterity, they have only one intention: to keep their ideas alive and provide the same as information for further generations to come.

Libraries have played a major role not only in accelerating the use of these different types of materials for information dissemination, but also studying these materials and developing more sophisticated technology for longer, faster and effective use. A better knowledge of information sources helps one to develop the right approach to collection and retrieval of information in a library setting so that information contents in these materials are better exploited and effectively utilised by the users in need.

Information is pervasive and available everywhere whatever form one may say. For one's communication convenience it can be better considered as sources with different types. Sources are the means by which ideas, opinions, facts and thoughts are communicated. Users are very often confused with the numerous sources of information available to them. The problem that is often encountered by a user is, how to select from the myriad sources, the information that is of most valuable to him. A knowledge of the information sources, their scope and limitations, their inherent characteristics, and the method of consulting them (easy or difficult) are equally important (Kawatra, 1989: p. 122).

The sources of information may be formal or informal. The line between formal and informal sources is difficult to draw, a reasonable approximation might be that formal sources are susceptible of use by a number of people not necessarily at the same time, while informal sources operate on an individual interpersonal basis (Ford, 1973: p. 87). Moreover, the formal sources are continuously increasing. Even unpublished sources are becoming increasingly important to scholars. Occasions will arise, especially in a special library or a university library, when information would be required by a user without pre-condition about the form of document. In such a situation, what matters is the finding of information, not the sources (Kumar, 1978: p. 98). However, it is needed to affirm from which source the information in need can be had.

Classification of Information Resources

While providing a number of information services and bringing out a lot of information products, library and information centres used to deal with several types of information sources. It is always desirable to group them into convenient classes in accordance with certain logical attributes. These attributes can be the publication process, target group, physical media, nature of presentation, information content, purpose, scope of treatment, etc.

Experts in LIS have shown considerable interest in classifying information sources into convenient groups. Guha (1983: p. 17), however, has described the division of documents as per the demarcation shown by Ranganathan, Hanson and Grogan.

Ranganathan's Grouping

Conventional	*Neo-conventional*	*Non-conventional*	*Metadocument*
Book, periodical, map, atlas, etc.	Standard, specification, patent, data.	Microfilm, audio-visual	Direct records unmediated by human mind

This categorisation of information sources emphasises the physical characteristics of the document. Another factor is that the documents are grouped in the chronological order of their development. It seems that this grouping does not cover adequately the information characteristics of the documents for a wider use.

Hanson's Grouping

Primary	*Secondary*
Books, journals, reports, patents, theses, trade literature, standards, etc.	Abstracting, indexing journals, citation indexes, subject bibliographies, reviews, surveys, etc.

This two-level category of documents of Hanson is an improvement over the previous one and seems to satisfy the users as well as the librarians to some extent. Because of the fact that the classification of documents is to be on the basis of level of reorganisation. However, it has not completely satisfied the requirements in a scientific manner. A question has been raised here: How can a textbook be considered as a primary document? Textbooks are assimilated information written for a particular level of users, the information having been drawn basically from primary sources. Hence, it could have been placed in the secondary category or some other category.

Grogan's Classification

Primary	*Secondary*	*Tertiary*
Periodicals, research reports, conferences proceedings, patents, standards, trade literature, theses, manuscripts, government publications, correspondence files, feasibility reports, case studies, maps, charts, atlases, photographs, graphics, etc.	Indexing and abstracting services, reviews of progress, reference books (encyclopaedia), dictionaries, handbooks, tables, formularies treaties, etc.	Year book and directories, bibliography of bibliographies, textbooks, guide to literature, etc.

This type of classification of information sources by Grogan appears to be more pragmatic as it logically identifies the information characteristics of the documents. In classificatory terms, information content and its uses are more valued than that of its physical media.

According to his groupings, primary sources of information are those documents which have independent existence, containing new and original information or the reflection of new ideas, observation, and experiment. An article in a journal is the new and original contribution of the author/contributor. Again primary document can be attributed to the publication process, in which it is first published. A research monograph is the original thought content/outcome of research project of a researcher which has never been published earlier and which takes the shape of a book form for the first time.

Here 'secondary' is used in the sense of immediately derived from something original, primary or basic. It can be cited that indexing and abstracting services are publications containing bibliographical details of the articles, with or without annotations derived from primary journals, are considered 'secondary' publications.

However, the term 'tertiary' is used in the sense of occurring in or being in a third stage. These types of documents are usually compilations drawn from primary or secondary sources, organised and arranged according to a definite plan. Essentially, these are to aid searchers in using primary and secondary sources. Among this group are various sources like guides, directories, bibliographies that all lead to other sources of information.

Katz's Categorisation

In accepting the above grouping of information sources, Katz (1982: pp. 16-20) adds three main categories: (1) control; (2) access; and (3) directional type. The first broad class or form of reference source is the bibliography. This form is variously defined, but in its most general sense, it is a systematically produced descriptive list of records.

(1) *Control :* The bibliography normally serves the role of a controlling agent. It invents what is produced from day-to-day and year-to-year in such a manner so as to enable both the

compiler and the user to feel they have a control, through organisation of the steady flow of knowledge. The bibliography is prepared through research, identification and classification.

(2) *Access:* After the controlling function is done, the individual items are organised for easy access to facilitate intellectual work. All the access type of reference works can broadly be defined as bibliographies, but they may be subdivided as follows:

(i) Bibliographies of reference sources and the literature of a field, be either a general or a subject nature. Example: *Sheehy's Guide to Reference Books.*

(ii) The library card catalogues or the catalogue of numerous libraries arranged for easy access through a union list. Technically, these are not bibliographies but are often used in the same manner.

(iii) General systematic enumerative bibliography which includes various forms of bibliographies. Example: *The National Union Catalogue.*

(iv) Indexes and abstracts, though are usually treated separately from bibliographies, but are considered bibliographical aids. They are systematic listings that help to identify and trace materials. Indexes to the contents of magazines and newspapers are the most frequently used types in the reference situation. Example: *The Readers' Guide to Periodical Literature.*

(3) *Direction:* Bibliographies themselves normally do not give definite answers, but they direct users to the different sources for answers. For their effective use, the items listed must either be available in the parent library or available from another library system.

Source Type

Unlike the access type of reference work, they are synoptic. It includes encyclopaedias, fact sources, dictionaries, biographical, and geographical sources.

Agencies of Formal and Informal Sources

Agencies of information can be grouped under two broad categories, viz., agencies of formal sources and informal sources (Babu, 1994: p. 91).

Formal Sources

1. Libraries:
   (a) Academic Libraries;
   (b) Public Libraries; and
   (c) Special Libraries.
2. Information Centres:
   (a) International Information Centres;
   (b) National Information Centres;
   (c) Regional Information Centres; and
   (d) Local Information Centres.
3. Personal Books Collection:
   (a) Self, and
   (b) Relating to friend/colleague(s).

Informal Sources

1. Agencies of informal sources of information come under:
   (a) Suggestions from colleagues/friends;
   (b) Contacts with peers;
   (c) Off-prints from authors;
   (d) Journal clubs;
   (e) Technological gate-keepers; and
   (f) Corridor meetings at conferences.
2. Communication among big groups:
   (a) Seminars and conferences; and
   (b) Invisible colleges (information exchange groups).

In summing up the above schemes of information sources groups done by LIS experts, an integrated approach can further be taken to categorise them in a systematic manner. Organisation of information presupposes the essence of the need to know the users and their information-use patterns. Users of information are categorised according to their status, level of works, and areas they are involved in. Though the information need may vary from person to person, a general pattern of requirement exists among various groups of users. In general, the following four types of sources are used to suffice for the needs of the users in different circumstances. They are:

1. Current information;
2. Exhaustive information;
3. Everyday information; and
4. Catching-up information.

Reading Habits and its Impact on Information Acquisition

Literacy is that social phenomenon which is more or less interwoven with the fabric of the society in order to make people know about themselves and others, and aware of the society around them as well. One of the important characteristics of the literacy programme is 'reading', which assumes a greater significance in present-day society, because, reading is a human activity that drives one towards an intellectual world. Grey opines that reading influences the extent and accuracy of information as well as the attitudes, moral beliefs, judgement, and action of readers (Devarajan, 1989: p. 14).

In other words, reading is the concomitant activity of 'writing' and both the production of delayed messages with a degree of permanence, and the utilisation of symbolised speech as a means of conveying messages account for the accumulation of information in a controlled fashion that cannot be accomplished through the human memory alone (Daily, 1978: p. 87). However, reading is the art of interpreting printed and written words, which is considered as the basic tool in education.

Reading is primarily considered as a habit of high order. It is one of the most powerful and lasting influences on the promotion of one's personal development. Such a habit helps in building the morale of the personality. Regular and systematic reading sharpens perspectives of one's living, and thereby prepares him for an effective participation in the social and political life. Reading habit is, therefore, considered as an exercise to mind.

Almost all of our intellectual activities are centred around the reading habits. Because, our primary concern is to acquire knowledge and reading habit being one of the important ways, it is widely and differently practiced by human beings.

Objectives of Reading

Reading habit though entails several objectives, its purposes differ from person to person depending upon the circumstances. Users of a library are also of variety in nature as their needs differ in respect to the use of various reading materials of the library with multifaceted missions. This can be exemplified by the following objectives of reading:

1. to meet the needs of short-range, long-range, reference services through the help of reference librarian;
2. to consult with only reference material/source such as subject dictionaries, general dictionaries, encyclopaedias, etc., without taking any assistance from the reference librarian;
3. to avail current information in one's subject of interest;
4. to keep abreast of the latest publications that are of interest to one's specific needs;
5. to make a serious and exhaustive study on a specific topic of a particular subject;
6. to make oneself aware of the day-to-day happenings; and
7. to utilise leisure hours by reading some light materials for pleasure reading.

Processes of the readers may differ, but their primary goal is directed towards increasing reading habits, which can be culminated in the institution called library.

Libraries and Reading Habits

The unprecedented growth of publication/information has accelerated the growth of knowledge that propelled the reading habits considerably. Such a growth is so huge and gargantuan that it is not possible on the part of human being to keep track with a particular piece of information. Neither personal purchase nor borrowing can quench one's thirst for knowledge or information. So, emergence of library is the only panacea to solve the problem of reading can be attributable to an essence in the world of human knowledge.

Libraries store information in different forms, bring out reading materials in readable formats according to their variety needs of their clientele. While libraries create the real atmosphere for reading, these ultimately increase the reading habits of the users. Sharma (1978: p. 171) is of the opinion that the practice of using the library will make a man habitual of going to the library and then he will realise that his reading in the library is essential for him as other essential items like breakfast. This very statement truly signifies that the role of a library is an essential ingredient for one's sound intellectual existence.

Scholars in search of information always try their best to establish permanent ties with the library to promote their reading habits. Hence, reading habits of the user-community is generated, maintained, promoted and achieved by the library and information system.

Reading Habits and Information Acquisition

A library system is primarily designed to serve a community of users and to provide them utmost satisfaction. To satisfy them, their needs are to be fulfilled and to fulfil their needs, their requirements are to be assessed. This ultimately drives one to undertake a study of users in order to determine their reading pattern, habits, information needs and information seeking behaviour and their approach to information so that an effective library system can be built up. Hence, the study on reading habit of a particular group of users substantially moulds the library management to develop such as system with optimal satisfaction. Information acquisition as one of the vital activities of a library is primarily based on the needs and reading habits of a given group of users. Because, information to be procured is selected basing on the needs and reading requirement of the users.

4

Information Needs

Users constitute inseparable and indispensable part of any library and information system. The emergence of an information organisation is due to the very essence of the users. While all the factors responsible for the existence of a library and information system are directed towards proper and effective use by a specific group of users, the central question of library's effectiveness and efficiency is based on the users and their needs. It is often remarked that a library is basically a service institution designed to provide information services to fulfil the information requirements of the community. Libraries are service enterprises and service will be better if the nature and needs of clientele are known (Martin, 1976: p. 487). A shift has, therefore, been developed to emphasise the successful use of the libraries on the basis of information needs of the users.

How users are the central focus and research on users is the most significant aspect to an information system can be best illustrated by the following quotes on "information needs and users":

1. It becomes increasingly clear that the success of information services is more likely to be achieved through adjusting the services to meet the specific needs of an individual rather than trying to adjust the individual user to watch the wholesale output of an information system (Garvey et al., 1979: p. 256).
2. Effective transition into the information will require switching from information systems that are technology

and content driven to information systems that are user-driven (Mick et al., 1980: p. 55).

The recognition of users' needs in terms of users than that of system is the new agenda for the library and information scientists. This user-orientation practice phenomenon is the order of the day in the library environment that is ultimately propelled towards improvement of the information system. Hence, library-users appear to be the steering wheel of an information system on which the LIS scholars are more anxious to know their users.

It is pertinent to raise certain issues related to the essence and emergence of research on 'information needs' studies. Although information needs are a part of user studies, actual emphasis was laid on study of 'information' needs and information-seeking behaviour in post-1950s era. The Royal Society Scientific Information Conference (1948) undertook several surveys of user's information-seeking behaviour. During 1960s, the work of M.B. Line, Michale Brittain, Menzel and Paisley through various articles published in Annual Review of Information Science and Technology (ARIST) accelerated the growth of research work and literature on information needs. One important milestone in this area is the work of the University of Bath where the study on Information Requirement of Social Scientist, popularly known as INFROSS was conducted. INISS and DSISS were similar type of works that led the scholars to be motivated to work on similar line.

Similarly, the studies of Dervin and her colleagues, Mick, Wilson, Rohde, Cronin, and Renekar outlined the theoretical perspective on the study of information needs research and devised models for the improvement of the existing state of the information-user studies.

A survey of the literature on information needs and uses suggests that all these studies are primarily clustered around two essential spheres:

1. The focus is laid on user study with a shift of emphasis to information-seeking behaviour during 1950s. Attempts were

made to depict the characteristics of the users as a sociological group explaining information needs and how to satisfy them.

2. The second feature is directed towards information retrieval and information system design. This investigation is intensely concerned with information retrieval strategies that might assist the users in representing their needs, and with the development and refinement of information systems in an attempt to reflect the users' needs better (Itoga, 1992: p. 331).

Altogether, more than 1,000 information needs studies have been undertaken at either macro or micro level. In spite of the work done, the system improvement on the library environment has not been appreciably good. Researchers are more interested to focus on micro problems and undertake studies to alleviate the problem and bring a solution to the long cherished desire of developing an user-oriented information system on library and information environments. This impetus enables professionals and researchers to know more about their users and explore possible improvements related to user-system interface in their respective libraries.

The present information science has urged upon the librarians and information scientists to seek to understand the library users so as to come up within their information environment. Why information-seekers choose to exploit certain information resources while ignoring others or why they decide to abandon one type of inquiry in pursuit of another are some of the questions of considerable importance to the field and to society as well (Sandstorm, 1994: p. 414). It is a universal phenomenon that libraries are meant for service delivery to the users and to provide improved services to the community. It is, therefore, desirable to know their users, their needs and preferences for the documents and such other related materials. In order to achieve the objectives of developing a good library and information source system and to arrive at the target of designing the library system and services to suit the requirements of its target users, the last and most successful method perhaps is to study the information needs and interests of its users.

Information Needs: The Conceptual Framework

The concept of information needs is the outcome of the combination of two terms 'information' and 'needs'. To make a sensible analysis of the concept, it is necessary to identify the nature and meaning of the above two terms and their significance in connection with user studies approach. What is information and what is need?

Much has been talked about information from definitional and conceptual point of views in the previous discussions. However, in a restricted sense, information is a sensible statement, opinion, fact, concept or idea or an association of statements or ideas (Evans, 1981: p. 2). In a broader sense, however, information is something which is transmitted by the act or process of communication, it may be a message, a signal, or a stimulus. It assumes a response in the receiving organism and, therefore, possesses responsive potential... It is instrumental and it is usually communicated in an organised or formalised pattern, mainly because, such formalisation increases potential utility (Shera, 1972: p. 164). As regards to the second term, what is a need? Everybody is engaged in some other assignments that are significant for him. These activities are designed to achieve the target, whether he is a farmer, teacher, physician, bureaucrat or a journalist. All of them are so heavily engaged in their respective area(s) of activities that they necessitate the help of some other elements that bring success to their work, which can be termed as 'need'. In this connection, it can be assumed that these professionals more or less depend upon information to update their knowledge or to answer their queries of some kind or other. To be full-fledged or self-sufficient on one's view, there is a great necessity of adequate and appropriate information in right time.

This lack of self-sufficiency in one's part constitutes one's information needs. The information needs represent gaps in one's correct knowledge that makes him quite satisfied with a given situation or work environment.

According to H.A. Murray, a need is a construct that presents a force in the brain region. It leads to organised action (Kumar, 1989: p. 443). Kumar, however, opines that the term, 'need' refers to such a concept to what an individual ought to have and differentiates want as what an individual would like to have.

Thus, it is inferred that 'need' can be defined as a situation that requires some course of action, which leads to want and good directed behaviour causing the tension in the respective individual's mental sphere.

At the root of the problem of information-seeking behaviour is the concept of information need, which has proved intractable for the advanced, by Wilson in 1981, that is, need is a substantive experience which occurs only in the mind of the person in need and, consequently, is not directly accessible to an observer. The experience of need can only be discovered by deduction from behaviour or through the reports of the person in need.

The general concept of need is, of course, a psychological concept, since it refers to a mental state or states and a good deal attention has been given to the idea, its subjective character and the motivation for the expression of need or the psychological drives that result in the expression of the need. Information needs, thus, is a concept of human need. Information need "arises whenever individuals find themselves in a situation requiring knowledge to deal with a situation as they see fit" and that information needs arise in all aspects of everyday life. The home, the office, in relation with family or friends or the insurance company out of idle curiosity, or as a requirement of work (Chen and Heron, 1982: p. 5).

Information need itself is a psychological state, not a visible object or complex of symbols. An information need, therefore, is something not directly observable. However, it has a definite existence in the minds of the user at least, and so, it is useful to have a term by which one may refer to it (Cooper, 1972: p. 21). It is sometimes confusing within the association of two terms: information and need. This complexity can be traced back to the connotation of basic need, synonymous with other human needs. *The Encyclopaedia of Psychology* on human needs has divided it under three basic categories:

1. Physiological needs often called basic need for food, clothes, shelter, etc.
2. Affective needs (sometimes called emotional or psychological needs) such as, need for attainment, for domination, etc., and;
3. Cognitive needs (often called esteemed needs) for need to plan, learn a skill, etc.

Obviously, these three needs are interrelated, one giving rise to another, after having fulfilled one need, i.e., psychological need, it may trigger off affective or cognitive needs, which is a very common phenomenon taking place in human beings. These interrelationships, therefore, give rise to search for information towards the satisfaction of needs. Wilson (1981: p. 8) has sought to remove the terms 'information needs' from the professional vocabulary and speaks instead of "information-seeking towards the satisfactory of needs".

It is quite difficult at times to know much in advance whatever information/text an individual needs and desires from given library in order to fit his reading taste. Wilson (1968) has found that perfect knowledge of an inquirer's predilection and perfect knowledge of all the texts which could possibly be used by an inquirer would be necessary before the ideal set could be identified. Librarians normally provide documents on the basis of usual identification and selection by inspecting records of those documents that meet the needs. It is not a usual practice that they used to observe and explore the usefulness of the relative documents provided for reading. Although keeping records of all these events on the library settings is a phenomenon, its influence on the real library and information activities is least realised. The knowledge gained from these records-keeping methods does not help build up the library functioning. Neither is it used to mould, nor outline individual reading behaviour of the user. Other factors that contribute to this phenomenon is the traditional library functioning, staffing arrangement and training in librarianship.

Although users constitute the core of the library system, the responses received from them are not appropriately and appreciably utilised for the decision-making policies of a library system. Unless a mechanism of close-monitoring is developed, user-needs may not influence library policies for overall developments.

Definitions

Information needs has become the central theme in information science research in a design to improve the existing condition of the library and information system and has focused on new models of users-driven information services. Research shows numerous definitions of 'information needs' that have been given by authorities on several fronts. According to Dervin and Nilan (1986: p. 17), 'information need' has been defined as a state of needing anything the researcher called, information. Almost without exception 'information needs' have not been defined as what users think they need, but rather in terms that designate what it is in the information system that is needed. The definitions have not focused on what is missing for users but rather on what the system possesses.

There is a paradigm shift in the definitional problem of information needs. The emphasis is more directed towards users and their state of psychological attitude. 'Information needs' refers to a relationship which obtains between information and the information purposes of individuals. It is, therefore, an objective condition rather than a psychological state.

According to Guha, (1983: p. 46), information need is referred to a composite concept of different types of requirements and approaches to information. Information need is defined as "a function of extrinsic uncertainty produced by a perceived discrepancy between the individual's current level of certainty about important environmental objects and criterion state he seeks to achieve" (Atkin, 1973: p. 206). Ford (1980: p. 100), in other words, has defined 'information needs' as a conceptual incongruity in which the person's cognitive structure is not adequate to a task.

When a person recognises something wrong in his or her state of knowledge and wishes to resolve the anomaly (Belkin, 1978: p. 58), this very act refers to information need.

Kumar (1989: p. 415) states that information needs are identified as individual needs of user regarding information, which should be satisfied by the individual information system. Information needs as defined by Krikelas says that "when the current state of possessed knowledge is less than needed", when internal sense runs out (Dervin, 1977: p. 28). When there is insufficient knowledge to cope with voids, uncertainty are conflict in a knowledge area (home).

In definitional terms 'information needs' are the knowledge-bound requirement satisfying the use of a specific bit of information within a framework of definite purposes.

Information need is seen both as a subjective and relative concept existing only in the mind of the experiencing individual (Wilson and Streatfield, 1981). It may vary with different situations with emphasis on individuals' various perceptions and characteristics. For example, individuals need information depending upon the circumstances and purposes. Decision-making is that purpose guided by certain environmental factors.

Information need is embedded with the concept of information. The information content of the document and the perception of users towards his requirement is confined to the study of information needs. In users study research, the term is prominently identified for determination of a reality in information-use by end-users.

Factors Affecting Information Needs

Information needs are a mere psychological and environmental attribute confined to the users. As normally human needs are cropped up by certain circumstantial factors, information needs are also affected by certain factors.

Paisley found the following factors that affect information needs to a great extent:

1. the range of information sources available;
2. the uses to which the information will be put;
3. the background, motivation, professional orientation and other individual characteristics of the users;
4. the social, political and economic systems surrounding the user; and
5. the consequences of information use.

Information needs, according to Dhawan and Sachdeva (1986: p. 104) are also greatly influenced by certain factors like, work activity, discipline, availability of facilities, etc. It is viewed that the need is very often based on the hierarchical position of the individual. The higher the position of the individual in respect of his scope of activity, the more information he needs to satisfy his requirements. A scientist having been in a senior managerial level looking after administrative affairs of the scientific organisation is running after information on management of science and technology rather than as science and technology information only.

Different professionals have their specific needs. A scientist at lower level is looking for information primarily on a new specific task assigned to him. Hence, his information need is confined to a narrow area of subject speciality. On the contrary, a teacher in journalism, whose basic objective is to train a breed of young people for the profession never looks for information on an event of investigative issue; rather he seeks to know how best to teach the students about the effectiveness of investigative journalism for practical purposes. Thus, higher the position, greater the facility and broader the scope of works that entail greater information.

The information needs of human beings, therefore, are greatly affected by the environment in which they work.

Types of Information Needs

Organising information at any level presupposes the essence of a need to know the users and their information-use habits. In order to determine the varied needs of the users, it is essential to identify the type of users before any attempt to assess the need is made. Users of information are of different types ranging from a child to an aged, illiterate to a highly educated intellectual, and a common man to a research scholar. People working at these scope of activity and level of understanding require information to satisfy their needs. Several studies conducted in the field have shown that information needs vary from person to person at different points of time and place. Although there is a common pattern of information requirement found among the various group of users, there is an exception in specific cases with a group of specified individuals. However, information need in all these cases are highly complicated. In order to arrive at a clear picture of information-users, it is always essential to demarcate the types of various information needs. Information needs have their own categories based upon different characteristics.

Based upon information-seeking behaviour, needs have been categorised as: (i) immediate, or (ii) deferred or distant (Krikelas, 1983: p. 8). Further, depending upon the stage of activity, types of needs can be identified (Martyn, 1974: p. 31) more effectively.

Normally, two types of information needs are identified. These are: (i) applicational needs, which are primarily concerned with finding answers to specific questions on problems, and (ii) nutritional needs, which are more concerned with maintaining the general competence of the individual matter than the needs proper.

Herner and Herner (1967: p. 22) have identified two types of needs. They are: (1) substance or kinds of message, and (2) means or channels of delivery.

However, Itoga (ibid.) while grouping information needs on different fronts and counts has considered the following three basic categories of needs on the pretext of human understanding as described below:

1. Perceptional Understanding;
2. Normative Understanding; and
3. Contexual or Subjective Understanding.

Perceptional Understanding

Information is provided to the users only when the provider perceives the users' behaviour, gestures and words without knowing any communicative meaning.

Normative Understanding

It happens only when normal communication is used to express the desire for a source by the user to the information provider.

Contextual or Subjective Understanding

It is the occasion when the information provider interprets the users' expression for sources within the meaning in context term in a simultaneity form. Cronin (1981: p. 40) has, however, considered the various information needs under three broad groups. In his practical experience, he could come across the needs for information as:

1. Expressed information needs;
2. Unexpressed information needs; and
3. Delitescent or dormant need.

He further adds that the users of information services may have information needs, which they are totally unaware of, but which the information provider may be able to bring to light.

Weigts et al. suggest the following categories: need for new information; need to elucidate the information held; and need to confirm information held. Here, it may be noted that the focus of these types is cognitive need, and given the significance of beliefs and values, it is required to add: need to elucidate beliefs, and values held, and need to confirm beliefs and values held, since information may be needed to achieve these things.

The modus operandi of carrying out of searches also identifies underlying information needs. For example, Carter (reported in Chew, 1994) suggest that when an individual is driven to seek information as a result of "needing to know" three modes of questioning behaviour are exhibited: (i) questions to discover what is happening (orientation); (ii) questions to check that the person is "on the right track" (reorientation); and (iii) questions to form an opinion or solve a problem (construction).

Approaches to Information Needs

The literature on information needs and users covers the fundamental terms in a different manner that do not define the concepts interchangeably. In order to provide a clear picture of the phenomenon, Dervin and Nilan (1986: p. 10) have enunciated the following six basic approaches to information needs:

1. Research approach;
2. Awareness approach;
3. Like-dislike approach;
4. Priority approach;
5. Community profile approach; and
6. Interests, activities and group memberships approach.

These approaches seem to find the strategical issues of information needs and assessment that paved the way for different patterns of use. The problem concerning the user-behaviour in relation to needs is very often judged by the system definitions of the needs. There is a limitation of user-concentration within the system. Hence, the resultant phenomenon is 'system needs' rather than the 'users needs'.

Information Needs in Information System Design

In regards to information needs the literature of computing and information system design appears to be deficient. This may be due to the fact that the system designers are not very much concerned with how information is processed, but with how computers are used. Veryard found a typical approach and sees the problem of determining information needs as being a mater simply of augmenting the system designer's normal data analysis model. The acquisition of data on information needs is described in terms that suggest that it is unproblemetical. It is essential to have interviews with the users at various levels either individually or, collectively to discover the decision-making and control processes they are responsible for, the performance measure they use, and the needs they have for information. The next step is to undertake an analysis of information needs with a representative sample for detailed analysis. Each selected information need is to be analysed in terms of data model. It requires a right research method to find out how the concept of information needs is responsible for designing and developing an information system.

5

Information-Seeking Behaviour

Human being is involved in certain social activities that are complex and interdependent. This phenomenon gives rise to increasing need for information from some potential sources that are not known to them. Moreover, the needs are myriad, and the variations among people are of different nature with regards to context, intellectual level, frequency, and volume of information sources required. Besides these, there are a number of institutions, organisations, and learned societies, industrial firms, government, and non-government agencies dealing with a variety of information in acquiring and disseminating.

With the growth of information deluge, each one needs information of increasing variety and diversity of level, frequency, volume, and use. This complex situation appears to be ambiguous and heterogeneous in character so that information needs of a particular group of users and information-flow from a specific situation/organisation are difficult to determine. Again, the use of information is so complex that there cannot be a simple system to cope up with the task of effective retrieval without assessing their specific needs. This situation has given rise to the growing concept of information searching and the manner of determining the pattern of searching is said to be considered information-seeking behaviour.

Users and their information-use studies perhaps form the largest single body of research literature in librarianship. Crawford estimates that well over 1,000 user-behaviour and information system user studies have appeared in print (Krikelas, 1983: p. 5). The recent developments in the field have added new dimensions to the research literature. It can be expanded by new approaches to citation studies, automated searching, text-retrieval and scaling of bibliographical databases. The body of literature on 'user-behaviour' within the framework of librarianship is increasing day-by-day.

This incessant growth of various aspects of the subject has led the researchers to concentrate more on service aspects in order to refine the services or redesign the information system. To crystallise the situation, different roles played by the users appear to be essential for an early assessment. Because, such an assessment would result in improving the existing system and generating new ideas and thoughts related to information products and services.

Information environment primarily appears to be critical as it involves users of information, organisations, information mediators, library and information centres, publishers, and producers of information. In this complicated situation, the role of the information intermediary assumes greater importance due to the fact that the intermediary bases the whole system upon the effective retrieval of information.

The present scene has given birth to the deluge of information and the complexity of centres or storehouses in such a manner that the role and responsibility of the intermediaries has been very much ambiguous and varied in nature. One can term the intermediary as 'information specialist' who helps people to find information they are looking for. Every activity related to information acquisition to dissemination is more or less an event that implies an information system finding out about, and producing the information required in that particular case. The intermediaries help the users to build up this system not only with their knowledge about storehouses of information, but also with the knowledge about the information-seeking behaviour of the users.

Normally, all library activities are designed to develop a system based on a string of services to be provided to the users upto their utmost satisfaction. In this connection, it can be summed up that "satisfaction out of services is the end and the library and information system is the means". On this premise, it can further be argued that the intermediary is more concerned with the provision of satisfaction of the users. Because he/she is directly dealing with the users to develop the system and it is essential to know the users and their information privations before information is rendered to them and new services are designed.

The librarians and information scientists have to be more concerned with the needs, i.e., 'information needs' of their respective clientele as has been elaborately discussed in the preceding pages. Once information needs are developed, the user has to develop the personal strategy of searching information from various sources. Thus, the concept of information-seeking behaviour of the user is being generated within a given library and information environment.

Current research on information retrieval and dissemination pays greater attention to the study of information habits and needs of users about myriad information systems. It has also been said that the user should be viewed more broadly as existing within interacting cognitive, emotional and social systems (Summers, Mathews and Conry, 1982: p. 75) while considering the user as the central focus of 'information needs', the emphasis is shifted on the personal and psychological attributes of the users that would provide a good understanding of the dimensions of the study. Hence, the emerging concept of information-seeking behaviour becomes the focus of the question, which needs a detailed emphasis.

Information-Seeking Behaviour: Theoretical Framework

A librarian's major task is to satisfy the users. In order to undertake such a critical task that involves a clear understanding of the psychological, physiological and social factors of the human nature/beings, one has to develop a deep understanding of user-librarian interaction based on human behaviour, which often remains unpredictable and complex.

If one looks deeper into the information sphere, the understanding of human involvement is more a factor that contributes to the existence of the system. In that, the attribute, personality and motivational structures that constitute the overall 'behaviour' of the human being is seen. A person needing information develops certain behavioural options. There are five main classes of these options: (i) to wait; (ii) to act; (iii) to generate information; (iv) to seek information; and (v) to opt out of the situation (Christie, 1981: p. 150). Each of these classes can be broken down into fixed groups and eventually into the specific concrete options available at a given point of time. But the general classes apply at all points of the behaviour structure.

The user can wait before deciding what to do, can act on the information retrieved so far, can generate information, can seek information, or can opt out of the situation, if the same does/does not suit to his taste or need.

Human brain acts as a processor of information. Zweizig in his work utilised the model of the individual as an information processor. Bell's (1991: p. 8) study analyses many information-processing mechanisms in animals, which are applicable to human being and provides a foundation for understanding searching strategies and tactics, patterns of resource distribution, and trade-off between competition and risk on time minimisation and energy maximisation. Charg and Rice (1993: p. 250) have further clarified the Bell's model of ecology influencing animals' searching behaviour providing some insights for the development of human behaviour theories.

Researchers in communication and psychology have shifted their move to view 'persons' as active and purposeful assets. As a result, human cognition and behaviour have become increasingly a matter to be discussed and applied as a mechanism for information processing, social and cognitive psychologists have developed a number of common concerns within this type of information-processing framework regarding such issues as the nature of cognitive structure, verbal memory, the processing of movies and visual information, impression formation, and stereotyping (Sypher and Applegate, 1984: p. 310).

However, information is not only an element of learning, but also is a set of stimulus for those human beings, who consider it as the sustenance of their sound existence. Those who like learning and knowledge, their attitude to information is equally electrifying their activities. Descartes has argued that only some human action stemmed from material and mechanical sources and information being the most vibrant material develops certain behavioural patterns in the human mind for a concrete action to be undertaken. Hence, the need for information and its seeking pattern is a genuine characteristics.

Information-Seeking Behaviour: Definitions

The phrase 'information-seeking behaviour' has been defined variously by different authors. The following definitions of information-seeking behaviour will, however, make the concept more clear.

According to Krikelas (1983: p. 7), information-seeking behaviour refers to "any activity of an individual that is undertaken to identify a message that satisfies a perceived need".

King defined information-seeking behaviour "as a manner in which a user conducts himself in relation to a given information environment. It is, therefore, regarded as essentially, a process of interaction between the user and the rest of the information system (Manda, 1991: p. 18).

The act of searching or finding information can be ascribed to information-seeking. Such an activity begins when the user perceives that the existing knowledge is less than that needed to deal with some problem(s). With the end of that perception, the process of seeking ends. Developing an instinct for information is a sort of behaviour and the process of searching the same is considered as information-seeking behaviour.

One can ask, "what is the basis of seeking?" Seeking arises when there is some perceived need. It is required to determine why individuals selectively seek certain kinds of information while they ignore or reject others. Based on Festinger's cognitive dissonance theory, it was suggested that individuals seek information that confines their pre-existing opinions, attitudes and favours their predisposition (Rahim, 1990: p. 100). In this same framework, it is noted that individual's information-seeking behaviour is not guided by the relative importance of relevance of an issue, but rather by their pre-existing attitudes towards the issue.

On the other hand, Hawking and Daly (1988: p. 202) have added selectivity process of dissonance theory. They have viewed that the selectivity process is not only a cognitive phenomenon, but it should be viewed interactively with other variables such as emotions, availability of information and specific domain of information.

The work of Donohew et al. (1990: p. 11), 'knowledge gap' contended that what motivates individuals to seek information is the relevance of such information to individual situations. Persons having higher social status or educational attainments are better equipped with information, but those who actually obtain from an information-seeking environments are seldom considered the least knowledgeable.

Factors of Motivation in Information-Seeking

There is a varying degree of motivation to seek information. It primarily depends upon the work situations or level of requirements or organisational factors. Individuals with this motivation to seek information on politics may not have the same degree of interest to seek information on scientific research/ or on investigative journalism.

Goldhaber et al. (1978: p. 82) suggest that persons are interested to seek information concerning their work environment. The motivation to seek information lies in information itself. Persons seeking information about job-related matters are very often motivated by the desires to get rewards for successful performance. Individuals will not be motivated to seek such information because of the same is perceived, that being reinforced.

Individuals' referent criterion or past experience also contributes to their information-seeking behaviour. The presence of a referent criterion would reduce the degree of probability of individuals' seeking information, because the need for new information is minimised (Grunig and Dibrows, 1977: pp. 145-67). They contend that the stronger the involvement, the higher the probability that individuals' would seek information about the situation.

On a study of a health information system, Etteme et al (1983: p. 525) find that circumstantial factors as predictors of information-seeking would not be powerful enough to generate active search for information, when such information is not readily available. In situations, where information related to the specific issue is readily available, individual situational factors would again emerge as better predictor of information-seeking.

Individuals in the course of time may exhibit different information-seeking behaviour, because of a significant difference in the nature of the problem. Certain jobs and lifestyles may be characterised by the degree of constraints they happen to face. There can be two types of situations in which information is consulted: (i) continuous, and (ii) discrete. Bureaucrats, for example, while dealing with specific issues face discrete problems. But journalists whose responsibility is to report in a daily manner need information continuously. The distinction is in the predominant nature, and this predominance may manifest itself in a general pattern of information-seeking.

How the users, especially, scholars use the resources and that is their usual habit of seeking information has been the concern of information intermediary. The same is being studied from a variety of perspectives. It is the responsibility of not only library and information science, but also the sociology, psychology, and cognitive science and communication studies. Increasingly, ethnography documenting the behaviour of individual scholars in their teaching and research environments will provide needed context for such work. Limited progress in explaining and predicting human information-seeking, retrieval and use, however, may be attributed to a lack of agreement about whether appropriate goal is to develop general or restrict investigations to descriptions of specific cases (Sandstorm, 1971: p. 418).

There are different dimensions of behavioural assessment, while some emphasise the sociological approach as the appropriate one, others prefer psychology or cognitive science that leads the behavioural patterns. Some still say communication system to be the mainstay in shaping the behavioural designs, while others consider observable behaviour or actions of the information-user that mould the human information-seeking behaviour.

Elements of Information-Seeking Behaviour

Information-seeking is a matter more or less related to the sense making, in which the individual chooses an item of information that best fits to his needs and purposes.

Making an in-depth study on information needs, Dervin and Nilan (1986: p. 12) have proposed a paradigm shift for information-seeking behaviour. They have identified an automative set of premises and assumptions, the essence of an alternative paradigm in a set of six elements. They are:

1. the conception of information as objective versus subjective;
2. information-users as passive recipient or objective information versus purposive, self-controlling, and sense-making beings;
3. user of information on behaviour applied across situations versus behaviour understood as the result of dialogue between system and user, in which need articulation goes through situationally bound interactions;

4. the study of user-behaviour primarily in the context of user-interaction with the system versus holistic approaches that focus on the whole social interaction;
5. focus on external behaviour versus internal cognition; and
6. concerns that a focus on individual behaviour yields too much variation for systems to integrate versus the need, with individuality in user-behaviour. They, however, conclude that traditional approaches have aspired to sophisticated quantitative techniques... yet in the context of the impetus of the paradigm shifts, scholars are now calling for supplementing quantitative approaches with inductive and qualitative approaches (ibid.: p. 16).

Information-Seeking Behaviour versus Gratification Theory

The gratification theory on information-seeking behaviour developed by Chatman (1991: p. 42) identifies the underlying methods by which researchers are able to explore a minimally understood area in information studies. The theory has attempted to define problematic situations for poor people and new conceptual factors that influence their choice of a strategy. It has attempted to address a central issue of information-use among poor people, even though they do not appear to be active seekers of information.

This theory illustrates immediate gratification behaviour that appears prevalent in the lower-working class. The findings suggest that no information-seeking will occur if respondents are convinced that good future is more attributed to luck, rather than to one's investment of time or energy.

In his attempt to determine the information-seeking strategies of engineers and scientists, Wolek (1972) made a study which is designed to assess their behaviour patterns when they need to enrich their understanding of a technical subject prior to an interpersonal communication (Christie, 1981: p. 159). The study has identified three basic methods of information-seeking: (i) piggy backing; (ii) friendly consultation; and (iii) professional peripheration. These factors are responsible for the methods to be adopted. Firstly, an user would tend to piggyback-giving information search a low priority if there were higher priority demands on his/her time. Secondly, a person would be guided by previous experiences, especially in regard to selecting appropriate sources of information. And finally, professional peripheration tended to be used when an understanding of the context of question/problem was felt necessary (ibid.: p. 160).

Holland's (1972: p. 160) study hypothesised that special communicators would be regarded by their colleagues as having especially high value as information sources and in term would have exposure to both a greater number and a greater diversity of information sources. In his result, he has suggested that the relationship between these two variables is usually very complex. Particularly, a number of variables like location, status, experience, telephone and travel budgets normally affect both information potential and information exposure.

Categories of Information-Seeking

People seek information in different ways and for different purposes. Thus the method of information-seeking varies from person to person and situation to situation. Lonnqvist (1990: p. 200) has identified the existence of two types of information-seeking:

1. Specific information-seeking with subject acquaintance of the scholar.
2. Dependent information-seeking when the subject is new and the scholar is not aware.

While the scholar is well aware of the subject, one can undertake information-seeking in a specific way that suits his/her needs. That is to say, one can gather references to literature on the subject in a specific time frame. One can also use the method of chain searching to choose the right track. This can be considered as the greatest skill in information-seeking which is normally practised by experienced scholars.

The second type is confined to either scholars started to work on a new subject or a new research project which is not known to him, or the user is not mature enough in terms of use of information sources.

The above two types of information-seeking do not always occur in their present form. Individual variations could be seen, but it is fair to say that these two main types crystallised.

While studying on reading phenomenon of secondary-school students, Harwood (1973) identifies seven main categories of information-seeking (Christie, 1981: p. 249). These are: (1) reading; (2) consultation: personal contact with the authority; (3) consultation: personal contact with non-authority; (4) thinking: vigorous; (5) thinking: intuitive; (6) systematic observation; and (7) casual observation.

Models of Information-Seeking Behaviour

A social researcher, before making an in-depth progress on the problem in hand, usually demonstrates his curiosity in order to ascertain whether any of his predecessors had carried out research similar to his problem, and if so, any model or theory to that effect has been established. This curiosity not only helps the scholar to conceive an idea during his initial stages of research, but also cautions him about the expected problems, which this scholar might encounter during the course of his investigation. Besides, such models sometimes act as path-finders. Thus, a question is frequently cropped up in the mind of a researcher as to why do people prefer particular source than others. Although there needs research into the matter to explore the truth, still it can be a common reply that the individuals select the sources that would be possibly a relevant material that contain required information with ease of access. People have several preferences for seeking information. Even if, it is very often based upon certain hierarchies. One can presume that given a choice, individuals prefer to get their information from a knowledgeable and perceptive source (i.e., one that knows the subject and understands the situation (ibid.: p. 16).

Users seek information at different situations on different circumstances. What is the behavioural implication related to information-seeking is a matter that needs detail discussion.

It can best be illustrated and examined by a couple of models developed by experts on user studies and information-seeking behaviours. The models described below represent information-seeking behaviour.

Early models of information-use were more conveyed with document-seeking or library-use than with the characteristics of behaviour. These works are confined to the use of the library systems and use of various types of documents. Very little is known about developing dynamic models of behavioural patterns of the information-user. As a result, adequate coverage and direction could not be established on the development of information systems.

However, a change was witnessed in which researchers have sought to use models based on the information-user as an organisational member and as a performance of different kinds of tasks, with different kinds of needs. With the advancement of library techniques, use, development of information system and services, a close look was given to the information needs and information-seeking behaviour. In spite of the narrowness of the research base, several in-depth studies were conducted in specific subject areas to determine the users, their information needs and specific traits of information-seeking behaviour of the users through development of suitable models.

During the early 1900s, an economist, George Stigler, had developed optimising models of information-seeking, in which he proposed the use of the concept of utility maximising behaviour to assess the quantity of information people would acquire at different levels of cost and effort: "the optimum amount of search will be such that the marginal cost of search equals the expected increase in receipt, strictly parallel to the analysis of buyers (Schwartz, 1992: p. 129). Stigler's theory, the "law of diminishing returns in information market", among other things is primarily considered as a significant contribution for which he was awarded Nobel Prize in 1982. Many social science researchers and authors have utilised his idea in their research work.

Similarly, satisfying models concerning to information-seeking designed by Simon in the 1970s emphasises the extent, to which individuals and groups simplify and terminate their work on a problem, not for reasons inherent in the logic of the problem, but for practical constraints (for example, time, money and patience). Simon was also awarded Nobel Prize in Economics in 1978 for innovating such approach to decision-modelling (ibid.: p. 130).

None of the above two models seem to hold any real prospect for generating a cumulative, theoretical framework about information-seeking behaviour. This is, economic models are rarely, if ever focus on psychological principles of optimal effort in information-seeking for which a paradigm shift on developing behavioural models are found.

Krikelas (1983: p. 17) has presented "the alternative model" to information-seeking behaviour. Though his model does not elaborately or specifically discussed information-seeking behaviour, its ultimate value lies in its utility in the design and analysis of future empirical studies.

However, the models developed by Mick et al (1980: p. 348-351) on management-oriented information research appears as a very pragmatic towards describing and studying information behaviour. In their description of 'individual behaviour model', they observed individual information behaviour in a corporate environment, where they could identify factors affecting individual information behaviour into a form for suitable policy-oriented approach to user studies. The individual behavioural model assumes that there is an internal, consistent logic, which governs information behaviour. That logic is the product of task requirements and constraints, perceived utility of various information sources, and the criteria for successful accomplishment of the task (ibid.: p. 348).

This model provides a perceived list of potential actions in response to a task, a style function, on evaluation function that provides feedback to the style sub-programme based on the response to behaviour.

In their attempt to develop a new model for information behaviour, they found a generalised model of scientific and technological information-seeking. The conceptual version of this model shows that a stimulus generated within the context of a particular situation, which occurs within an environment and a set of attitudes that generate an information need. A general plan of action is generated in response to this need resulting in a specific action. Once the specific action is performed, its results are evaluated and results of the evaluation provide feedback to attitude and need. This model is used to guide the exploration of the relationships among variables affecting information behaviour.

Robert's (1993: p. 472) 'information man' model is more applied in classical economics, where it predominantly plays a major role in economics than on information studies. As he pointed out typically, information man does not have an analytical role, even within limited information environments. His functions are as implicit as his presence. Assumptions about what constitutes behaviour have influenced both the direction and the kind of research undertaken; the problems studied in effect, are indirect reflection of information man. They are no less substantial for being unacknowledged. It is unusual to discover data being explained by resource to behavioural interpretation derived from assumptions held about such behaviour.

Although 'information man' is a simple and conservative for the purpose of study, it shows an epitome of conceptual sophistication compared to major extent models of information-seeking behaviour used for information retrieval research.

In the grounded theory approach, Ellis (1993: p. 473) has propounded a behavioural model of the information-seeking patterns of academic social scientists. This model was employed to recommend for information retrieval system design. Further studies were also concluded modelling the information-seeking patterns of academic and researchers in science and literature at the University of Sheffield.

Wilson (1981: p. 9), however, has a different but pragmatic view on discussing a model. In his opinion, human personal needs are at the root of motivation towards information-seeking behaviour. These needs emerge due to different roles an individual plays in social life. The 'work role' is most important, which is applied in different activities, responsibilities and achievements of an individual, especially in an organisational setting. The work role generates some cognitive needs, which again leads to affective needs. The ultimate result is the emergence of a pattern of information-seeking behaviour.

Information-Seeking Behaviour in a Digital Environment

With the growth of information deluge, each one needs information in increasing variety and diversity level, frequency, volume and use. This complex situation appears to be ambiguous and heterogeneous in character so that information needs of a particular group of users and information-flow from a specific situation/organisation are difficult to determine. Again the use of information is so complex that there cannot be a single simple system to cope up with the task of effective retrieval without assessing their specific needs. This concept has given rise to the growing concept of searching and the manner of determining the pattern of search is said to be considered information-seeking behaviour.

With the advent of information and communication technologies in libraries and their massive use, the pattern of information-seeking behaviour appears to have experienced a changed phenomenon. The users of traditional libraries and their patterns of searching information are different from that of digital libraries. The range and method of satisfying information needs varies from a traditional library to an electronic library. The succeeding discussion gives a complete analysis on the shape of information-seeking behaviour in a digital information environment.

When a user comes to library, he has narrow ideas of information sources and marginal behavioural approaches. While he establishes an interaction with the information intermediary, he gets the knowledge of several pertinent sources and his attitudes develop into a very good pattern of seeking behaviour. Similar is the situation in the web-based information-seeking.

The growing popularity of Internet has given ample opportunity to the users to browse a large number of sources. While surfing the net, users find several digital information objects of their choice, whether directly or indirectly useful to them. This pattern of viewing the net is developed in to a behavioural model of information-seeking on the web as combined by Augilar's modes of scanning and Ellis' seeking behaviours. They have identified mainly four modes of information-seeking, as such, indirect viewing, conditioning viewing, informal search, and formal search. The study made by Catleige and Pitkow on the web browsing behaviour found that the web pages that the users book marked did not match the most popular sites. Only 2 per cent web pages were either saved or locally printed. They hypothesised that users in their study categorised as browser spend less time on a web page than searchers.

Web information-seeking may be influenced by web browser functionality that makes it easy to go back to recently viewed pages. Touscher and Greenberg showed that overall users only access to a few pages frequently (60 once, and 19 twice) and browse in very small cluster of pages. It is interesting to note that web browsing activity is recurring system, where users predominantly repeat activities they had invoked before, while still selecting new actions from the many that are possible. In a recent study, Huberman et al. (1998) identified several strong regularities of web-user surfing patterns and developed a mathematical 'law of surfing' that determines the probability distribution of the depth, that is, a number of pages a user visits within the website (p. 95). They developed a 'strong fit' model that predicted the number of requests for each web page on a web site by which a more robust understanding of information-seeking patterns on the web. The model finally proposes to the existence of utility maximising behaviour underlying surfing.

People use the web as an information storehouse to support their research activities and to meet day-to-day information needs. The mode of information-seeking on the web depends on the nature of information needs. Information-seeking tactics, and the purpose of information-use. The most important factor of determining the behavioural framework is the motivation and the method of information-seeking. The availability of web-based information resources and successful operation of search engines guides the behavioral pattern of information-seeking. Users find it quite interesting and useful to browse the web than to search the library documents. Hence it can be concluded that the web-based information search has influenced the users since it is congenial in a digital environment.

Information-Seeking Behaviour of Working Journalists

Working journalists appear to be dedicated information-seekers since their sphere of work is totally confined to information-flow, their routine jobs are heavily engaged in the retrieval, repackaging, processing, and dissemination of information. These activities provide rich data on the information behaviour of the working journalists and the interactive relations between the information system and information-users.

Working journalists are those professionals, who primarily seek information to improve their quality of reporting and feature writing. *Guardian*, a major British newspaper defined characteristics of working journalists' information needs and information-use models, as well as information sources. There are two types of search: the fact finding search and the background search. In fact-finding search, they usually depend on formal information sources. But, while searching for background information working journalists would seem to be quite willing to delegate searching to the media librarian, providing that the search is conducted quickly, efficiently and successfully (ibid., 1987). While using informal sources of information, their own experience, memory and telephone were largely used for seeking information.

The researches found that the newspaper library in a metropolitan daily newspaper had been recognised as a major source of information and ideas in the production of news. The contents of old issues of newspaper, whether stored in a paper clip format in rows of filing cabinets or electronically, help journalists meet information needs. In addition, the reference collections and staff of the news library played an important role. With the availability of new information technologies in the news library and throughout the newsroom, there is great potential for change in newsroom routines. In particular, the role of the news librarian as contributor to the news process has come into sharper focus (Ward, Hansen and Mclead, 1988)

Foley and Brisco, while emphasising the scenario of large metropolitan newspaper libraries gave a detailed guide of what and how a news librarian should do to meet the journalists' information-seeking needs in such an environment, compared with the traditional news librarian. News and information sources, which can be accessed directly to the end-user without the journalists as an intermediary, would change their relationship between consumer and the provider of content and consequently bring an alteration of journalist's information-seeking activities. Journalists now might change their working from method to content facing such a threat. Williams was on the track of old argument, but with new perceive journalists should refrain from using databases as their primary sources of information. The reason is being that when reporters relied on databases for their facts, they could get a story that is incomplete, inaccurate, or lacking in historical perspective. And sometimes they could end up with no story.

Benett (1995), a newspaper librarian, commented that the role of the news librarian should play significantly in the process of journalist's information-seeking and use. Again, he said that it was becoming increasingly de rigueur to hear that we information intermediaries get our kicks from standing guard between information and the people who need it. The author argued that such a rhetoric was driven by corporate tough times and a need to rationalise the downsize of the library. It was questioned whether reporters really want to be empowered to do their own research, especially five minutes before their deadline.

In order to understand the journalists' information-seeking and use of the information environment of the newspaper setting plays a significant role. Campbell and Johnston in a paper reported that as environmental knowledge is retrieved and interpreted by journalists, the emphasis and meaning placed on information is altered. While it agreed the findings of Rosamma Joseph (1993) on the issue of journalists' unawareness of the basic information retrieval and unwillingness to use formal information facilities, Campbell sought to establish a mode to describe the journalistic construction of news, using journalists of Scotland as data. The findings concluded that it was the newspapers itself, which determined how the news product was created. So did the features of information-seeking behaviour by the working journalists.

The post-1996 period witnessed a changing phenomenon of research in the studies of information-seeking and use by journalists. It is due to the very fact that the advent of electronic information environment, especially the widespread use of Internet, had a great impact upon the use of information by media persons. The focus was shifted to the relationship between the Internet and the news media. The work pattern of the working journalists changes and also the analysing structure of information needs and information-seeking and use also drew some attention. The next chapter succinctly discusses the changing scenario of journalists' information needs and information-seeking behaviour in an electronic information environment.

Research on Information-Seeking Behaviour

Research on information-seeking behaviour is on the rise. With the growth of multidisciplinary subjects and interest of researchers of new micro subjects, there appears a tremendous increase of special users in libraries and information centres. To cope with the task of providing satisfactory library and information services, it is always desirable to make a close look at the information-users. Hence, library intermediaries have started to undertake several research works on information needs and information seeking behaviour of their users at different levels.

As mentioned in the previous chapter, more than 1,000 studies have been conducted in the areas of information needs, uses and seeking behaviour. In spite of such voluminous work done one's understanding of the process that drive information-seeking or the variables that influence is limited or inadequate.

While commenting on the problems of user studies in the previous two decades Brittain (1982: p. 147) aptly concluded that:

> Always the number of user studies had increased greatly during the 1900s and 1970s, resulting in an enormous quantity of data about the information gathering, seeking and using behaviour of a large number of scientists, applied scientists, social scientists, practitioners, administrators, government officials, school teachers, educationists and finally, the members of general public, there were no generally acceptable theoretical guidelines to make sense of this huge mass of data.

Saracevik (1987: pp. 24-25) while speaking on information-seeking, however, has characterised the current state of knowledge of cognitive aspects of information-seeking and information retrieval in terms of two basic questions: (1) at the level that the nationalists used to ask a hundred years or so and (2) that concerns not only with identification of the variables, but what is their nature and their effects?

The situation remains same as Krikelas reacted to Saracevik in the words "work in this area of information-seeking is so arduous, because we are only now beginning to understand how complex the process may be and how difficult it is to define, let alone measure many of the important concepts (ibid.).

Most importantly, the publication, *Annual Review of Information Science and Technology*, while providing a series of reviews on "information needs and uses" has contributed a lot to the research discourse on information-seeking behaviour. Attempts have been made to relate specific variables to particular pieces of information-seeking behavioural patterns. A good number of articles have also been presented which are devoted to in-depth analysis of behavioural components of information-uses. Still a renewed endeavor seems imperative in order to discover some of the important issues that remain hidden and possibly unexplored.

Theory of Cognition and Behaviour in LIS Research

While the physical sciences deal with matter and property of various kinds within the confines of a laboratory, social sciences primarily consider human being and its surrounding as its field of study and research. The LIS users are considered as one of the most vital elements for the research work. Because the interaction of the users with library and information system is the key issue that helps the system to grow and work effectively. In this connection, it can be discerned that the attitude and researcher's knowledge on cognition and behaviour to LIS research becomes crucial.

Human as Information Processor

Human being has sensory receptors like eyes, nose, ears, etc., that pick up signals of different kinds at different circumstances. These signals are information that are transmitted to the processing unit called, brain. The result of the processing is output/responses in the form of physical, spoken, written, etc. Although the capacity of processing information in human is limited, it produces effective solution to problems. Information processing in human being is being catalysed by the concept 'cognition' whereby, the output appears to be highly purposive, effective and refined.

Cognitive Theory

The term 'cognition' is an ambiguous term. It has meant different things to different people at different times. *The Oxford English Dictionary* lists several meanings of cognition including the action or faculty of knowing. Some other concepts, with which cognition is associated, include awareness, comprehension, skill and, understanding (Benjafield, 1993: p. 3). Cognition has a place of prominence in psychology and it has got a branch called 'cognitive psychology'.

Cognitive psychologists have propounded some theories related to cognition. Among these Peak's theory of psychological structure is used in a very common sense approach to refer to a system of relationship between identifiable episodes. The organs of the structure may be psychological traits, complex concepts having different characteristics, speech, symbols, etc. These components of psychological structure are located in a spatio-temporal manifolds, and are related to each other in many different ways. Behaviour appears to be the phenomenon that leads to a change within or between structures. Peak's analysis emphasises the condition that influences the probability of activation the psychological structures (Lindzey and Aronson, 1968: p. 321).

The implicative and international character of cognitive theory has been developed by Ablesen and Rosenberg (1958). They considered the elementary units of cognitive organisation to be cognitive representation of this concrete and abstract and to which individuals can attach verbal levels. They proposed a three-fold classification of element types:

1. Actors: oneself, other people groups, etc.
2. Means: actions, instrumental responses, etc.
3. Ends: outcomes (final products).

These elements can be connected by four types of relations, namely, positive, negative, null, and ambivalent. The elements and their relationship from the cognitive units that help people in knowing, perceiving for conceiving a particular thing through the development of a faculty at the mental stature distinct from emotions and volition.

Since a library is designed to provide services to multifarious users, it is essential to know the different personality traits of the users so as to determine their behaviour patterns. Cognition plays a vital role that influences the users' attitude towards the use of library materials. Again, it effects the information needs and information-seeking behaviour of the users to a great extent.

Thus, it is imperative on the part of the researchers of LIS to depict a thorough view of the cognition and its different aspects that have a different direct bearing on the human being in using resources of libraries.

Behavioural Approaches

The term 'behaviour' refers to any activity of a living organism, human or sub-human. It may consists of a simple overt or covert responses. Runkel and McGrawth (1972: p. 174) define behaviour as a real world event involving overt and covert responses by one or more actors to a task and situation. It said that a child knows how to walk, or ride a tricycle. The evidence is simply that the baby and child exhibit the behaviour specified. Moving from verb to noun, one can say that they possess knowledge, and the evidence is that they possess behaviour (Skinner, 1974: p. 151).

Behaviour exists only when it is being executed. Its execution requires a psychological system, including effectors and receiptors, nerve and brain. The system was changed when the behaviour was acquired, and this is the chain system which is 'possessed'. The behaviour it mediates may or may not be visible at any given moment. There are parallel in other parts of biology.

Knowledge is associated with behaviour, be it verbal or non-verbal behaviour, the concept of information theory is applied wherein a message is sent through the form of sound stream between the speaker and the listener. The transmission of information from one person to another has been used metaphorically to represent the transmission of input into output. As a form of knowledge, information can be treated more effectively as a behavioural repertoire.

Hence, the term behaviour stems out from the internal need for information that corresponds to the external environment of the human being. Here, it is apparent that behaviour towards information becomes an essential element that constitutes one of the major ingredients in the study of information needs and information-seeking behaviour of the user-community.

A library, which is very often described as the storehouse of knowledge and information, deals with users of various kinds. It moulds the behaviour of the users at different points of time depending upon the available resources, technology and expertise of the professional intermediary. The physical environment of a library attracts the users and repels too. While users are the central focus of the library and information system, their attitude and behavioural pattern appear to be not only interesting but also essential in determining their specific needs and in designing a suitable information system and services. Hence, it is imperative on the part of library intermediary to render adequate importance to the cognitive and behavioural aspects of its clientele so as to put its resources to optimal use.

6

Information and Communication Technology (ICT) in Journalism and Mass Communication

The last quarter of 20th century witnessed the dawn of another revolution that is popularly called 'information revolution'. Information has tremendously influenced every walk of human life. The emerging computer and communication technologies have revolutionised the use of information in all its ramifications. The effects of this revolution have far-reaching consequences on the socio-economic aspects as well as the quality of human lives in the present society.

The ICT is a confluence of several technologies, such as, computer, telecommunication, semiconductor technology, fiber-optics, photonics, cellular technology, satellite technology, advanced networking, improved human computer interaction, and digital transmission and compression technology. These technologies help in a bigger way towards processing storage and dissemination of information which are the basic functions of ICT.

ICT in Newspaper Libraries

The ICT has attracted the attention of media persons in a very big way. The use of computer has been widely available in major operations of newspaper organisations. But libraries attached to big newspaper organisations have also started to use computer in storing, processing and disseminating information in a formal manner as happened to research libraries. The electronic library systems have proved to be of use for journalists in seeking information to improve the quality and contents of their news-reporting. After the edition of a day, newspaper is printed, the copy goes to the library for permanent storage, preservation and further use. The back volumes of newspaper started in paper clip format or electronic format help the working journalists to meet their several information needs. The basic needs of journalists include fact-checking and background information that gives the value and readability of the news item and the story becomes interesting. The traditional method of handling information in the news, library poses problems for the journalists as well as the librarian. With the present emerging technology, the news libraries have experienced radical changes in their operations. Also, the newsrooms found it quite interesting in its operations in using ITC. In the event of the technological changes, the computerised library operation's help the newspaper libraries with a solutions to many of their concerns since automated system could offer the power of on line information retrieval to journalists and editorial staff previously limited by manual information files. The system would enhance both the ability and speed to fulfil expressed information needs.

The year 1985 appears to be the milestone in newspaper library automation. A paper estimated that more than 50 newspapers were started to use electronic system to store and retrieve the newspaper's contents with installations expected to double in the next one year. The resultant effects were upon the newspaper libraries in which 100 newspaper libraries installed their electronic library system. The availability of online databases drew more attention of researchers to the system among the end-users. Well-run newspaper libraries of the past, with all their problems, still provided solid information in a timely manner to the media-users. But the trend toward computerised library was irreversible. Traditional libraries are doing typical work on demand during the day as an adjunct to using the library's own collection, rather than as the first line of response. In automated news libraries, the librarians must use their search skills constantly to respond to most of the questions they received. A study clarifies that it was exciting mixture of yesterday's newsprint traditions, tomorrow's electronic technology, and today's deadlines that makes news librarianship dynamic and rewarding.

The first news library automation appears to be held in *New York Times* Information Bank that offered index and abstracts to articles in computerised form. This led to other news libraries to start hybrid systems involving computerised indexes of news articles available on easily searched microfilm. During early 1980s, major news libraries in western countries started their own full-text retrieval system. The period also felt the need for-automation of library information services in newspaper organisations. Chepesiuk confirmed the study of Hensan and Ward and found that the electronic library systems have become not just norm, but necessities at many large and medium-sized newspaper libraries. The trend has brought dramatic changes in the way news librarians do their jobs and how they relate to the newsrooms. The library had been called as the news research library or editorial information centre, an indicator of the library's increasing importance. The resultant phenomenon was that the newspapers had begun giving their librarians bylines on the significant stories as credits. It was again confirmed that as reporters and editors gradually learned to handle the complexities of online searching, the future role of librarians might be in uncertainty.

In order to provide specialised information services to journalists, there was a need for software and the firms started to develop software relating to news libraries automation. Large-sized newspaper establishments adopted technologies that created their electronic libraries. Journalists and editors attracted to have easy access to databases that contain full text of several newspapers and other related information required in journalism and mass communication. The newspaper libraries began to create their own in-house databases of local investigation reports that appear to be hot issues. The library staff do not clip stories from the daily editions, rather they use video display terminals and access the computerised versions of the published news items.

Databases in Newsroom

With the emergence of computer and communication technologies, the reporters find it worthwhile to use information technology (IT) in newsrooms. By using IT, the journalists try to tap into entire files into their own terminal. It has the benefit of accumulating the wealth of information collected at all levels of government and use that information to assist the reporters. In order to facilitate the electronic accumulation of information, they find the need for databases to be created by news librarians in which the computer assisted reporting makes reporters easy to access to those databases. There are basically two types of databases that are useful to the reporters in the newsroom. The first is existing databases of commercial online services in which full text of newspapers and magazines can be accessed. Another form of database is in-house database for internal use.

Accessing commercial databases through online method is possible to access large reservoir of information in different areas/subjects that journalists may like to use. For example, Mary Kate Learning of the *Palm Beach Post* relates how her news library beat the competition on early census stories with the help of the Census Bureau's on Line File, CENDATA. Some county governments have extended the facilities of allowing remote dial-up access to their mainframe computers and to the public information stored there. *The Daytone Daily News* and *The News and Observer* are among newspapers gaining access to county records such as real estate and property tax, register of deeds, and voter registration data. These can lead to a few supporting paragraphs in a story or to breaking an entire story (Ripley, 1991).

Creation of in-house databases in newspaper organisations serves several useful purposes for journalists. It is the function of the news librarian to create databases, store them and disseminate information to media-users. The contents of databases may be the news item, feature articles, editorial columns, collection of photographs, and, statistics, etc. Newsrooms can also use database techniques to track off information from other sources and the flow of that information. Joseph Hallinan of the *Indian Polis Star* created his own free-text database to help him analyse insurance report narrative for a Pulitzer Prize winning series on medical practice. *The News and Observer* created a database for a two month project that brought together the work of six reporters, two editors, a photographer, graphic artist, press designer and news researcher. For this four-days series about an industrial accident in North Carolina, the news research department designed a database on a programme for legal case analysis, and used it to organise and access a more that a hundred files of reporters' notes and news coverage from other media (Leonard, 1992).

Storage of Electronic News

In newspaper organisations, it is essential to store news for a longer period so as to facilitate the further use by media persons. There are several methods of storing the news in electronic formats, out of which the following three suitable ways are discussed. News can be stored in full text without any additional subject analysis. This is typified by NEXIS, the service offered by Mead Data Central. News can be searched by headline, byline, date, place of origin, and name of publication. Any word in the body of the story can be searched. But one cannot search by subject.

Another method of storage is to prepare controlled vocabulary. In this method, it is possible for conceptual searching, because human analysis has been added. The disadvantage is that the intervention was human and there is lack of consistency. Another ways of storage in electronic format is to add enhancement terms to the text of the story. This is used in the Vu/text system. Words such as major story, opinion, analysis commentary, and statistics are added, because they help the searcher understand the kind of story that is available. Here, there is also the problem of inconsistency. The advantage of enhancement is that modern journalistic prose strive to be different. In contrast to the hard sciences continue to present problems in language control. Looking as how best to handle semantic confusion, news content analysis will have to find the best of two worlds. Free searching of full text can turn up the needle in the haystack.

The other method of quick searching is to expand on a system the old Infobank offered. If one desires biographies of a person, he/she can enter the keyword 'bio'. If he needs reviews, he/she can enter the word 'Rev'. Number or alphanumeric codes can be assigned to a restricted list of common types of news stories and letter to the editor. Such codes a common in business and financial databases. Information Access Corporation's (IAC) newspaper and magazines database do not offer major newspaper full text. The bibliographic citations include in-depth indexing using Library of Congress (LC) subject heading plus a special field of descriptors. This field had to be added because it proved impossible to intelligently analyse daily news using LC subject headings. The IAC products are available on Dialog and NEXIS. Dialog is a powerful and popular commercial database that offers a wide range of subject-oriented databases that can easily be used to supplement the IAC database when necessary.

Microfilming in Media

The use of microfilm has significant importance in media organisations, especially to preserve the newspapers for posterity. Microfilms are the most durable medium of information storage, which can last almost 1,000 years. This appears to be the most suitable method of archival preservation for media organisations. Newspapers are the excellent documentary objects for microfilming for a variety of reasons. Newspapers are normally oversized reading materials and need a lot of space for storage. These are often kept usually in basements, which hasten deterioration. They are frequently used documents since they contain a lot of information in variety of areas. Such a heavy use may cause rapid deterioration of newspapers. In order to avoid such physical decay of newspapers microfilming appears to be the best method of permanently preserving for posterity. If one goes to find the advantages of microfilm, the followings are appropriate merits:

1. It is the substitute for the original and provides a service copy that saves wear and tear on the original documents.
2. It provides long-term preservation of historical records, of which newspapers form a significant part.
3. The reduction of physical form can come to 90 per cent of the original documents for which the library can save a lot of space
4. In comparison to other types of restoration treatment, microfilm is relatively inexpensive.
5. Microfilm helps in easy retrieval, if indexed and classified, especially for newspapers.
6. From security point of view microfilm appears to be the best method to avoid theft and mishandling.

Although microfilm has advantages, it has also disadvantages. The following are some of the demerits:

1. High quality reproduction of documents from microfilm cannot be assured.
2. It is difficult to make paper copies from the film, although reader-printers are improving all the time.
3. Other accessories are required to make use of reading and printing of materials.
4. It is uncomfortable to use film reader in which there will be stress on the eyes if used for a long period of time.
5. Without good register or indices, the film is almost impossible to use.
6. The conversion of documents into microfilm form is costly and expensive.

Internet for Journalists

Internet has become a buzzword now-a-days. In most of the offices, research institutes, libraries, the use of Internet has become widespread. The use of Internet has become so common that there is no necessity here to give an introduction on it. However, one can say that Internet is a network of networks which is used for sharing and dissemination of information using a communication software. Internet consists of numerous disjoint information sources and is called as global storehouse of information.

Internet provides different services such as e-mail, mailing list, usenet, telnet, file transfer protocol, etc. The succeeding paragraphs describe the use of Internet for the journalists. Although e-mail is a common method of sending messages for those using web, it appears to be the most useful mode of contacting for journalistic purposes. It is due to the fact that journalists have least time to take in sending messages through postal service. While the basic purpose of journalism is to bring to the masses investigative news by interesting reporting, the use of Internet can add value to the news item prepared by the journalists. The reporter interested to prepare an interesting story can take the help of web to browse similar types of stories taking place in global sphere to make his story interesting. Journalists in order to improve the quality of their news-reporting find the use of Internet, in fact, checking and background information. If a reporter is investigating a crime incidence, he can browse through Internet what type of similar crime events have been occurred earlier elsewhere so that he can cite in his report to make a worthwhile news. Citing good instances may increase the quality and readability of the story.

A journalists may know science, technology, economics, sociology and an expanding list of other areas. It is difficult on one's part to be conversant to every discipline. But the use of Internet can make a professional know that subject in detail if he is interested to use Internet regularly. A journalist interested to browse the news organisations over world can connect them and find information about their working, set-up, editing procedure, circulation, specialisation, etc., so that he can acquaint himself with the modern trend of journalism.

The development from computerised on-line information system to the Internet had great significance for the journalists as well as the news librarians. In order to successfully implement ICT in news gathering and reporting, a number of researches have been undertaken at different levels. The following discussion gives succinctly some of the research projects taken up in this regard.

The use of computer and related technologies during late 1980s in newspaper organisations has created wide avenues for computer-assisted reporting. The newsrooms were digitised. Efforts were taken up to develop statistical and relational database programmes that could be used on desktop computers in journalism. An electronic environment was created in the newspaper organisations, in which a change in the computer-assisted news-gathering, production and reporting was experienced that altered the modes operandi of the working journalists.

Computer-assisted reporting at different newspapers was studied by Garrison (1997), who reported the findings of three different national surveys. It studied the current status of online resources and reviewed three year period from 1994-96. It noted that while much of the focus was clearly on global communication using the Internet, particularly the World Wide Web, the same was facilitated through the online tools. Many of these were highly specialised and served the needs of journalists as information-gatherers. These tools had also experienced growth in use in the past three years. Journalists had learned that these on-line tools were time-savers, generally more through and extended the reach of their reporting skills. Though sometimes costly, the expenses incurred were justified compared to other more conventional procedures and the efficiency achieved. Another report of Garrison(1997) analysed the subject of newspapers most often published using computer-assisted reporting. The focus was on both routine daily stories and special projects, and findings were based upon two national mail surveys of daily newspapers conducted in early 1995 and early 1996. The study found that local and national crime statistics and education were the most often named subjects, but the judicial system, local public spending, traffic tickets, elections, and campaign contributions were common subjects involving computer-assisted reporting. Topics for news stories that used on-line research included company or business profile, crime and the courts, education and financial securities, etc. Background information, finding experts, searching for people and sources, checking other newspapers' news stories and accessing on-line databases were among the most cited uses of on-line reporting tools. Although three were some variations, not a significant change was witnessed while studying for list of topics for both the years.

The findings of the study entitled "Journalism and Internet: the Changing Information Environment" by Williams and Nicholas (1997) showed how the Internet was impacting the information environment in the newsroom, with special attention to journalists and librarians. For journalists, they already had more than enough information, tight deadlines, and very little space to express themselves. For news librarians, the Internet had arrived and it was seen as a positive force in their work. At the library of the *Guardian*, it was used as a matter of course. Therefore, the fieldwork in the form of in-depth interviews indicated that news librarians were much more positive about the Internet than the working journalists colleagues, but were more aware of the problems, such as that of the authenticity or validity of retrieved data. Finally, it was suggested that the Internet, despite being considered an end-user tool, would create a new and important role for the information professionals in the future, including the possibility of involvement in more primary sourced investigative work.

Another research project "Journalism and Internet" was taken up by Nicholas, Williams, Cole and Martin (1997) to discover whether the Internet represented the paradigm shift for the information world by surveying 200 journalists, editors, and news librarians. The study found that despite what happened to be the considerable and direct benefits for them, probably less than one in five national journalists use the Internet-the proportion is much less than that for regional journalists. Firstly, the Internet was supposed to be a run-away hit with end-users beguiled by its power and simplicity, not so. Secondly, the Internet-user profile does not conform to the stereotype that young graduates were to flood the workplace expecting to use the Internet, not so. It turns out that the average Internet-user is middle aged, established, and often with editorial responsibilities. Thirdly, the Internet issues, which information professionals have flagged as being important, such as information overload, hardly concern end user journalist at all.

7

Journalism: A Contemporary Scenario

Journalism: The Notion

Human communication is as old as humanity itself. It is not certain when human beings started to follow a particular device or system of exchanging messages. But it is normally understood that the oldest form of human communication is non-verbal. With the rapid growth of science and technology, several forms of communication system began to develop. One of the most remarkable results of the industrial revolution was the emergence of mass communication and the 20th century can appropriately be considered as the real age of development of news media. To Vilanilam (1993: p. 167), "mass communication is just an embryo in the womb of contemporary human history. Perhaps, it will abort itself or be aborted by the very forces which engendered it".

Mass communication is perhaps considered as one of the major influences on society and also one of the most complex of human phenomena. The relevance of communication to human problems became so vibrant that it has generated a number of branches through which the problems can be better focussed for alleviation. Of all those forms of mass communication, the print media appears to be the most prominent as its components—the press and the newspapers—are worldwide considered as the 'Fourth Estate' where the society is totally reflected with its images.

The essence of the concept 'Fourth Estate' is eminent due to the very existence of a group of people called, 'journalists'. The profession they belong to is popularly known as 'journalism'.

The concept of journalism, however, appears to be somewhat in a considerable state of influx and complex. The term 'journalism' is derived from the French word *'journey'* (day of work) and in turn from the latin *'diurnal'* (daily or recurring everyday). It indicates the collection and periodical publication of current news or events or the business of managing, editing, writing for journals or newspapers on recurring basis. The use of the term has broadened in recent years that includes news-reporting and commentaries on radio and television and to lesser extent motion pictures (*Encyclopaedia Americana*, 1983: p. 218).

The term 'journalism', according to Parthasarathi (1995: p. 1), is both an art and profession, which records events and opinions and seeks to interpret and mould them for the benefit of public. To Wainwright (1992: p. 1), the term 'journalism' denotes information, news, and communication (mechanics). These two concepts perhaps inspired Wainwright to define the term 'journalism' as the event of the day distilled into a few words, sounds or pictures processed by the mechanics of communication in order to satisfy the human curiosity of a world, which is eager to know what is new.

The new *Webster's International Encyclopaedia* (Harkevy, 1991: p. 581), however, viewed the term 'journalism' as an activity that involves preparation of information for communication media including newspapers, magazines, radio, and television. Thus, the concept 'journalism' appears to be a clustering of several words such as information, events, communication, investigation, news and views, reporting, editing, and the alike.

The basic tenet of the early journalism is the 'freedom of the press'. With this noble idea, the progress of the concept has been spectacular over last few years. Since it has rooted with the phenomenon of public opinion, the widespread support given to the field has widened its horizon. As a result, new and varied dimensions of journalism have emerged. With the passage of time, a long road was developed from print media to electronic media, in which the term 'journalism' became the mainstay. Journalism, which was earlier confined to newspapers and magazines, got new impetus at the emergence of communication and IT. Journalistic activities are greatly attracted usually towards modern technologies, in which the efficacy of journalism is tremendously improved. The widespread and highly used television and computer technologies have facilitated journalists to reach the people much faster their door-steps with their first-hand news. And this is due to this emerging phenomenon, the term 'journalism' became more popular, wider, and responsive among the masses.

In a wider perspective, today's journalism has demonstrated the need of much more than just acquiring newspaper editing and reporting expertise. Mass communication today consists of several interdisciplinary areas such as, anthropology, economics, information science, political science, public administration, psychology, sociology, etc. In addition, the study of journalism and mass communication deals with kaleidoscopic media theories and communication research pertaining to process, impact of propaganda, advertising, publicity, public relations, radio, television, development communication, films, inter-personal communication, VCR/VCP, satellite communication, publishing, computer technology, the Internet, and many more.

The pivotal role it plays in reforming the society has brought the attention of all. In this context, the people working for the media claim to have a profession called journalism. There is a hot controversy regarding the professional status of journalism which is succinctly described in the succeeding paragraphs.

Journalism as a Profession

The social responsibility in journalism is entrusted to a group of people, who used to do yeoman's service to the society. Those people, who come with a missionary zeal to serve the public, are usually considered to be fit for journalists. This ultimately tends to consider the profession of journalism, as a noble one. Rau (1968: p. 36), therefore, finds journalism as a profession with its own technique, its own tradition and its own sense of fellowship, and viewed that as a profession, it has survived the assaults of commercialisation. He further quotes the views of the first Royal Commission on Journalism profession which states that

> there is still a widespread sense of vocation among pressmen, they feel a call somewhat as sailors feel the call of the sea, journalism is like seamanship, it cannot be without professionalism.

The professional status of journalism has, therefore, been a matter of great controversy and needs an in-depth study and debate. Perhaps, one of the core objectives seldom laid down by many concerning to journalism is that any one can conquer this profession without even any formal education in it. It has been found time and again that there are cases of expert journalists doing excellence in their field without having any formal education, which cannot be found either in medical or in legal profession. Porter (1968: p. 265), however, of the strong conviction that by the conventional definition of the word 'profession', the occupation of a journalist cannot be construed as a profession in true sense. Although an increasing number of practitioners have received their training in some academic institutions or other, no such formal training is required either to secure a job or to fit it well. He observes further that even some of the highly successful journalists are found to have been men of slight formal education. Thus success of a journalist in the profession does not necessarily warrant formal education.

While discussing the sociological significance of this profession, Agrawal (1995: p. 14) aptly opines that journalism as a profession does not have its traditional counterpart in the true sense of the meaning and hence, it is a modern profession, a by-product of technical advancement with main emphasis on the dissemination of information to all.

It has been argued time and again that journalists do not belong to a profession as they are largely recognised merely by the importance of their work. They are having a high social responsibility for which they work and demand respect. This, however, being a generalised observation needs re-examination.

Sociologists, however, feel that although journalism is on the way to professionalisation, it has yet to attain the status of a profession. Professionalisation of journalism in the US, Britain and France from 1760 onwards has been examined by Nevins, who characterised the professional education of journalism into (i) achievement of freedom of speech; (ii) emergence of press as an instrument of public reading; (iii) development of individual leadership; and (iv) obliteration of this individualistic leadership (Mahajan, 1990: p. 119).

In a different analysis, the *Encyclopaedia Britannica* has commented that during the second quarter of the 20th century, the tradition that anyone could be a journalist first came into conflict with a growing sense of professionalism among workers for press and radio. Several important factors influenced this trend that the earlier organisation of working pressman, specialised education for journalism, and an increasing sense of social responsibility on the part of journalists, etc., were very much on the card.

Subscribing to the view of sociologists that journalism in India is on the way to professionalisation, Dubey (1982) contends that journalism started developing as a free profession during the British administration. It is clear that most of the Indian journalists are salaried employees and free-lancing journalism has hardly received any encouragement.

Scholars in support of journalism as a profession, however, convey a different view. In analysing the theoretical aspects of the profession, the noted sociologist Parson has viewed that "the development and increasing strategic importance of the profession probably constitute the most important change that has occurred in the occupational system of modern societies. The growth of the profession has brought to prominence, a set of occupations, which never figured prominently in the ideological thinking that after having crystallised in the late 19th century, has tended to dominate public discussions in the 20th" (ibid.: p.14). This clearly indicates the growing acceptance of journalism as a profession.

Social scientists have determined certain key attributes of a profession that make same an ideal one. These are: (i) specialised knowledge; (ii) norm of altruism; (iii) authority; (iv) autonomy; and (v) monopoly. Here, it can be examined whether the profession of journalism fulfils these attributes.

Although quite a good chunk of journalists in India are working without having a formal training in journalism, there is a growing consensus that the field is in great need for certified professional training in journalism in India. To be a member of the profession, one must have a compulsory professional training, which is considered vocationally relevant and essential.

Journalists are highly respected in the community due to their close affinity with social responsibility. The First Press Commission Report of 1954 has demarcated that the responsibility of regulating the profession is left to the journalists themselves, they would not hesitate in enforcing a code of conduct, which would ultimately enhance the prestige of the profession and ensure that Indian journalism progresses along healthy lines (1995: p. 559). It is widely recognised that the press is a universal institution designed to safeguard the interest of the public and maintain a sound social order.

The question of professional authority and autonomy is apparent in journalism, which is non-existent here. As journalists are working for a common social cause, they do not have a particular client to dictate for authority. After all, they are working in an organisation for which they are responsible. This has reduced in exercising their autonomy as they have to often work along the line of their editor's ideology though not absolute. Again, the monopoly of journalism indicates self-control of professional journalists over their own affairs and non-interference from other non-professional bodies.

The above description clearly indicates that journalists lack authority, autonomy, monopoly and altruism upto a significant degree in their modus operandi as well as working status.

However, journalism as a profession has been well claimed by the journalists time and again. This is due to the fact that the growing concern for journalism has been highly recognised in the society and journalists by dint of their responsibility to society are regarded as highly revered. Since journalism has a very short history of about 200 years only, phenomenon of professionalisation has started late. The question of professionalism in journalism is a debatable issue, which needs a detailed and empirical inquiry. However, notionally journalism is considered to be a profession is held in high esteem today in the political, bureaucratic, academic and, intellectual circles.

History of Press in India

In India, the practice of reporting as an act of transmitting message to the royal courts about the on-going activities in the state was a rule. During the Asokan period, the emperor had many sources of information through the spies to collect information about the various subversive and socio-religious activities of the people. The Moghul period saw the news writers *(Vaquianaries)* appointed in the various administrative units in their territory and were charged with the function of sending reports to the headquarters of the administration. These manuscript reports were submitted exclusively for official use, and there are early indications of such news writers those who were working in collusion with a governor or a local administrative official, presenting them in a favourable light to the central authority and covering up their tyranny and oppressive executions (Ahuja 1996: p. 1). Evidences show that some hundreds of such original news papers of the Moghul courts were sent by Col. James Tod in 1828 to the Royal Asiatic Society in London; the papers were measuring 8 inches by 4½ inches in size on an average, written in various lands, record notices of promotions, visits by the emperor, hunting expeditions, bestowal of presents and news of similar interests (Rau, 1974: p. 9).

The rule of East India Company (EIC) has also witnessed the concept of news-reporting that made use of extensively to report the affairs of the state. But this sort of news-reporting was primarily confined to the royal palaces for information of the emperor or the company's administration.

With the arrival of Christian missionaries to India with an avowed interest of propagating Christianity among the Hindus, spectacular changes took place in regards to press and newspapers. They set up printing presses for the first time in India to propagate their cult. Because, their realisation was that the press would be a powerful medium, through which they could reach the people and promote their vested interests.

In course of time, printing presses were established at different places in the country and publication of different types of documents was started. Although Indians condemned the act of setting up of presses due to their suspicion that Christian faith will be propagated resulting in the extinction of Hinduism. But subsequent events changed their attitude and it was widely accepted that press was a powerful medium through which the freedom of this country can be achieved.

It is interesting to mention that in spite of the printing press established during the 10th century, an instance of newspaper publication is delayed by more than two centuries. A little is known about the reason(s) for such an inordinate delay. However, an abortive attempt was made by William Bolts, an ex-officer of the EIC to start such a newspaper in Calcutta in 1776. While he expressed his intention that he had in manuscript many things to communicate which most intimately concerns every individual, he was ordered to quit Bengal, who then left for Europe (ibid.: p. 2).

The 29th January, 1780 is considered to be a red-letter day for the cause of Indian newspaper industry. It was James Augustus Hicky, who may be rightly called the 'Father of Indian Journalism', for the first time, published, printed and edited the first newspaper, *The Bengal Gazette* or *The Calcutta General Advertiser.* It is relevant to depict that the history of Indian press is deeply associated with the magnificent personality of Hicky.

The *Bengal Gazette* was a four-paged tabloid and the size of each page was possibly 39 x 28 cm of which the print area occupied 31.5 x 20.5 cm. With much hardship, Hicky started publishing his paper even without the availability of basic technologies such as, telegraph, telephone, telex, teleprinter, mechanical composing and the publication of this newspaper became a continuous one.

Recognised as the 'Father of the Indian Journalism', Hicky will ever shine as a beacon to Indian journalism. He has left his legacy to posterity—the freedom of press. The founding fathers of the Indian Constitution have enshrined his name by incorporating the freedom of speech and expression as a fundamental right to every citizen of India (Padhi and Sahu, 1997: p. 7).

Soon after the *Bengal Gazette*, publication of newspaper became a practice rather than a myth. The trend of publishing more newspapers was set in motion, which continued to operate with much vigour and dynamism. Hicky showed the route of techniques and procedures for others, which appeared most effective. Table 1 shows the succeeding publication of five more newspapers in Calcutta.

One of the interesting features of this publication process is that all those newspapers were published in English by Englishmen and were circulated among English people working with EIC. The last decade of the 18th century also witnessed the emergence of a large number of publications from Calcutta. Important among them were *Asiatic Mirror* in 1794, the *Calcutta Courier,* the *Indian Apollo* in 1795, the *Telegraph* in 1796, the *Calcutta Morning Post* and the *Oriental Star* in 1798, and the *Relator* in 1799. Thus, Calcutta became prominently known as the birthplace of newspapers and journalism in India apparently for its leadership in press.

Table 1

Five Important Early Newspapers

S.No.	Newspaper	Year	Place	Language	Editor	Publisher
1.	*Bengal Gazette*	1780	Calcutta	English	James A.Hicky	James A. Hicky
2.	*India Gazette*	1780	Calcutta	English	Peter Reed and B.Messink	Both of them under government patronage
3.	*Calcutta Gazette*	1784	Calcutta	English	-	Published under government patronage
4.	*Bengal Journal*	1785	Calcutta	English	Thomas Jones	-
5.	*Calcutta Chronicle*	1786	Calcutta	English	-	-

Source: Ahuja, B.N., *History of Indian Press: Growth of Newspapers in India*, 1996, Surjet Publication, New Delhi.

With the phenomenal growth of newspapers in Calcutta, the trend was already set in other major cities in India. *The Madras Courier*, the first newspaper in Madras came into existence on 12th October, 1785 at the initiative of Richard Johnson, a printer to government. It was followed by the *Madras Gazette* published by Robert Williams and *India Herald* in 1795 by Humphreys. Similar attempts were also made to publish newspapers in Bombay. *Bombay Herald*, the first English weekly started in 1789, followed by *Bombay Courier*, the forerunner of the present *Times of India* and in 1791 the *Bombay Gazette* was started.

The foregoing newspapers started in all the three major cities in India are mostly British in spirit and content. The publishers borrowed the principles and techniques of publication and the style of news presentation mostly from British newspapers. Hence, these newspapers primarily do not serve the purpose of India, as these are read by only Englishmen.

However, there came a spectacular change in the attitude of the Indians towards using and publication of newspapers. One significant move in this direction was the initiative taken by Gangadhar Bhattacharya to start a newspaper, *Bengal Gazette* in 1816. Though it was a short-lived one, it is justly remembered as the pioneer of Indian-owned newspapers.

Language Newspapers

The political awakening of Indian people led them to consider the existence of a newspaper of their own as the only instrument of public opinion. This idea became much stronger, which was reflected in the publication of language newspapers. The Serampore missionaries started in 1818, publishing *Digdarshan*, a Bengali language monthly magazine and in the same year J.C. Marshman started the *Friend of India*. Again, in 1819, J.C. Marshman published another weekly newspaper called *Samachar Darpana*, which continued till 1840. This was followed by the launching of *Bombay Samachar* in Gujarati Language from Bombay. Another significant contribution was the emergence of Raja Ram Mohan Ray into the field of newspaper publications. He started *Sambad Kaumudi* in Bengali and *Mirat-ul-Akbar*. With the pace of time, newspapers in other Indian languages began to publish in different parts of India, and the real growth of Indian newspapers thus occupied a pivotal place and gained more prominence after the independence.

An estimate shows that there is a significant improvement in the circulation of newspapers in the country. In the whole country, the total number of newspaper circulation as of 1992 has gone up to 31,957, the highest being 4,631 in Uttar Pradesh followed by 4,226 in Delhi, and the lowest being one each in the Union Territories of Daman and Diu, and Dadar and Nagar Haveli, respectively. The *Orissa* occupies 15th position in the total circulation of newspapers in the country, which is less than 2 per cent to national level. In Orissa, there is also a considerable improvement in the total newspaper circulation over past few years.

Table 2 below clearly depicts the scenario of the 10 leading global newspapers, by their circulation, while *USA Today* published from USA has been considered as the top circulated English daily with 15,29,064 copies, the *Chicago Times* from the

Table 2

Leading Global Newspapers

S.No.	Newspapers	Circulation	Country
1.	*USA Today*	15,29,064	USA
2.	*Daily Express*	12,19,591	UK
3.	*The New York Times*	11,48,849	USA
4.	*Los Angeles Times*	10,60,441	USA
5.	*Daily Telegraph*	10,54,314	UK
6.	*The Times of India*	9,45,600	India
7.	*The Washington Post*	8,16,474	USA
8.	*New York Daily News*	7,28,205	USA
9.	*Times*	7,24,839	UK
10.	*Chicago Times*	6,84,294	USA

Source: INFA Press and Advertisers Year Book, 1996-97.

same country occupies 10th place among the 10 leading global newspapers with 6,84,294 copies. The *Daily Express* from UK having 12,19,591 copies of circulation occupies second position among the 10 leading global newspapers. However, India does not lag behind much in this respect. *The Times of India* published from India (from several cities) having a circulation of 9,45,600 copies seems to have occupied the sixth place among the most leading circulated newspapers of the world. However, USA seems to have overshadowed the list of 10 leading circulated dailies of the world as it covers six out of 10 such newspapers; followed by UK 3 and India is having the remaining one. Apparently, it is the poor literacy rate that ultimately has placed India in the third position.

The newspaper circulation in India is a matter of great concern for all as has been depicted in the Table 3. As shown, while *The Times of India* is considered as the most circulated English daily both in urban and at all India level, *The Dainik Jagran* in Hindi language and *The Malayala Manorama* in regional languages, i.e., Malayalam from Kerala occupy top positions in respect of their daily circulation in All India basis. In respect to the circulation in urban areas, *The Punjab Kesari* a Hindi daily and *The A. B. Patrika* in Bengali language occupy top positions. Unfortunately, none of the newspapers in Oriya language figure even under top regional dailies in respect to their circulation, especially in regional basis. The force(s) that did not keep Orissa in the map of top daily newspapers of the country is that Orissa which constitutes only 3.7 per cent of the country's total population (3,15,12,000) accounts 57.68 per cent villages that remained below poverty line. State's 87 per cent population, those who live in villages, are not in a position to afford a daily which has ultimately lowered the rate of circulation of The *Oriya* daily.

Table 3

Topline Readership in India

Top Dailies: All India		
English	*Hindi*	*Regional*
The Times of India	The Dainik Jagran	The Malayala Manorama
The Indian Express	The Punjab Kesari	The Matrubhoomi
The Hindu	The Nav Bharat Times	The Daily Thanthi
	Top Dailies: Urban	
The Times of India	The Pubjab Kesari	The A. B. Patrika
The Indian Express	The Nav Bharat Times	The Daily Thanthi
The Hindu	The Dainik Jagran	The Eenadu

Source: INFA Press and Advertisers Year Book, 1996-97, p. 394 c.

India, being a multilingual state, poses numerous problems as well as opportunities for researchers to study its various focal aspects. As depicted in the Table 4, Hindi, as the mother-tongue, occupies top position in the language profile of the country as the same is understood by large number of people and read by 36 per cent of the total population. English, not having been the mother-tongue, occupies second position in respect to speaking and reading aspects. Oriya being a regional language is read by only 2 per cent of the total Indian population.

Table 4
Language Profile

Language	*Mother-tongue*	*Language Understood*	*Figures in %*
Hindi	30	68	36
Bengali	8	10	6
Telgu	8	10	4
Marathi	8	10	7
Tamil	7	8	5
Gujarati	5	6	4
Kannada	4	6	3
Oriya*	3	5	2
English	0	22	20
Others	27	39	17

Source: INFA Press and Advertisers Year Book, 1996-97.

* Since the study is confined to Orissa, it is relevant to depict the position of Oriya language national level, even if, the same is not available in the above source.

Communication plays an important role in the development of a nation. In Indian subcontinent, various media have contributed a lot towards several facets of development. How far the progress it has achieved in the last 12 years. While Television (TV) occupies the prime of place among all the media, Press holds the second position. Next to TV, newspaper is the most dynamic form of communication medium in the country. According to *INFA Press and Advertisers Year Book*, 1996-97, in urban areas, newspaper has reached to 48 per cent of the population whereby in the rural areas, the circulation of newspaper is not of much encouraging which is confined to only 13 per cent.

Growth of Press in Orissa

The impact of western culture made a tremendous change on the social lives of Oriya people. When the people of Orissa are dreaming for the development of an intellectual environment, the press, as an instrument of the spread of knowledge and wisdom, came to the soil of Orissa as a blessing. The Christian missionaries, in their attempt to propagate the Christian religion also established a press in Cuttack known as The Cuttack Mission Press in 1837. The great famine of 1866 had a disastrous effect upon the state. The precarious condition of the people knew no bounds, which the British Government then totally failed to control the situation. To overcome the said unbearable situation, the plight of the people was greatly affected by historic famine that the state had ever seen in its history. The need of a newspaper as the vital carrier of information was then felt essential at all quarters. A well-known Oriya youngman, Gourishankar Ray, started to publish *Utkal Dipika*, the first newspaper of its kind in Oriya language in 1866, which continued to provide its message till 1934 with many ups and downs.

The Oriya literature and language met its formative period during the second half of the 19th century. This period witnessed a critical situation not only by drought, but also by a cultural threat. The very existence of Oriya language, therefore, was a problem to many owing to non-existence of a separate independent state, thus the adjoining states had an adverse influence on the unified language for Orissa, especially the Bengal province, which had the severe impact on the culture of Orissa. Due to total indifference of the British Government and the strong influence of Bengali language, efforts were made to abolish Oriya language and substitute it by the Bengali language as the medium of instruction in the schools of Orissa (Samal, 1989: p. 111).

This had led to a strong agitation by which T.E. Ravenshaw, the then Commissioner of Orissa, who prevented the British authorities to commit such a grave mistake and recommended the use of Oriya language as a medium of instruction. Three literary celebrities, namely, Fakir Mohan Senapati, Radhanath Roy and Madhu Sudan Rao were the pioneers in the field of giving Oriya literature its modern shape. They revealed in their writings the profound influence of western ideas on their thought (Mansingh, 1962: p. 185).

Fakir Mohan Senapati, who has been regarded as the 'Father of Modern Oriya Literature', started a newspaper called *Sambad Bahika* in 1868 at Balasore. During that period one king Baikunthanath Deo also established a press and started a newspaper known as *Utkal Darpan*. They both became pioneers in the development Oriya language and literature through the publication of their respective newspapers.

Table 5

Some of the Earlier Newspapers Published from Orissa

S. No.	*Newspapers*	*Language*	*Frequency*	*Year of Publication*	*Place of Publication*
1.	*The Utkal Dipika*	Oriya	W	1866	Cuttack
2.	*The Sambad Bahika*	-do-	W	1868	Balasore
3.	*The Utkal Hitaisini*	-do-	W	1869	Cuttack
4.	*The Utkal Darpan*	-do-	M	1873	Balasore
5.	*The Utkal Putra*	-do-	F	1873	Cuttack
6.	*The Sikhayak*	-do-	M	1873	Balasore
7.	*The Swadeshi*	-do-	W	1877	Berhampur
8.	*The Oriya*	-do-	W	1879	Cuttack
9.	*The Mayurbhanj*	Oriya and English	M	1879	Baripada
10.	*The Purusottam*	Oriya	M	1887	Puri
11.	*The Sambalpur Hitaisini*	-do-	W	1889	Bamanda
12.	*The Ganjam News*	-do-	W	1896	Parlakhe-mundi
13.	*The Ganjam Oriya Hitabadini*	-do-	W	1899	Berhampur
14.	*The Star of Utkal*	-do-	W	1909	Cuttack
15.	*The Asha*	-do-	W	1914	Berhampur
16.	*The Samaj*	-do-	W	1919	Satyabadi (later from Cuttack)

W = Weekly; F = Fortnightly; M = Monthly

Source: Collected from different sources mainly on books devoting publication and printing history of Orissa.

Taking into account the effectiveness of the print media and the increasing awareness of the people about their language and reading habits, the trend of establishing more printing presses not only became very popular, but also imminent. During that period the presses like Mayurbhanja Press (1879), Bamanda Press (1885), Jagannath Ballav Press (1887), *Utkal Darpana* Press (1902) were established in different towns of Orissa (Tripathy, 1990: p. 22).

Those printing presses were primarily engaged in publishing newspapers and magazines with different frequencies. Some of the newspapers published during that period are mentioned in Table 5.

As has been described earlier, the missionaries were instrumental in setting up the presses in Orissa, they had also taken attempt to publish newspapers first. The following newspapers appeared to have been published by them:

1. *Gyanaruna* 1849
2. *Prabodh Chandrika* 1856
3. *Arunodyoya* 1861

Reverend Lassey had taken the charge of editing the newspaper *Gyanaruna*. The editors of the remaining papers were, however, not known. The foregoing newspapers were considered to be the missionaries' mouthpiece for propagation of their respective religion. As a result, they failed to cover the news in real sense and lost their popularity and subsequently ceased their publications.

A new era in the journalism history of Orissa started with the publication of two newspapers, namely, *The Asha* and *The Samaj. The Asha,* published and edited by Sashibhusan Rath made its first appearance in April 1914 from Berhampur and became very popular as a newspaper for which the publisher took the attempt to make it a daily newspaper in 1928. On 4th October 1919, *The Samaj* resumed its first publication from Satyabadi with the sincere efforts of the then well-known freedom fighter late Pandit Gopabandhu Das. The publication of *The Samaj*, the popular Oriya daily heralded a new age in the history of Orissa's newspaper and Oriya journalism to a considerable height.

The Samaj became extremely popular due to its contents and coverage being suited to the information needs of the people, particularly the rural mass. During that time, the freedom movement was very much on the card. This newspaper became the mouthpiece of freedom movement. Taking into account its popularity, the publication of the said newspaper was shifted to Cuttack in 1927 and was turned into a daily newspaper and since then, it has almost become as a household commodity in each and every Oriya family of the state.

The publication of another Oriya newspaper, *The Prajatantra* in 1932 established and edited by late Harekrushna Mahatab had tremendously influenced the literary and social lives of Oriya people. A new phase in Oriya journalism started with the publication of the said newspaper. After a long closure, it was again reappeared as a daily newspaper in 1947 and still continuing as a major circulated Oriya daily.

The subsequent publications of several other newspapers from different places of Orissa as depicted in Table 6 have enriched the language, literature and journalism in Orissa to a remarkable height in comparison to other contemporary states.

Table 6

Newspapers Published from Orissa
(in alphabetical order)

S. No.	*Newspaper(s)*	*Periodicity*	*Year of Origin*	*Editor(s)*	*Publisher(s)*	*Place of Publication*
1.	*The Agnisikha*	D	1968	A. R. Panda	D. P. Nayak	Sambalpur
2.	*The Aji Kagaja*	W	1984	Dillip Mohapatra		Angul
3.	*The Aji Kali*	D	1985	B. Mohanty		Balasore
4.	*The Ajira Khabara*	F	1983	S.N. Tripathy		Nowrangpur
5.	*The Aneka Suchana*	D	1991	N.N. Panda		Bhubaneswar
6.	*The Anupama Bharat*	D	1996	Sarat Mishra	R.K. Panda	Berhampur

Contd...

S. No.	Newspaper(s)	Periodicity	Year of Origin	Editor(s)	Publisher(s)	Place of Publication
7.	*The Bartaman Samachar*	D	1994	R.C. Nayak	R.C. Nayak	Bhubaneswar
8.	*The Bisesha Khabara*	W	1984	M.K. Swain	M.K. Swain	Bhadrak
9.	*The Bisesha Sambad*	W	1996	B.C. Choudhury	B.C. Choudhury	Bhubaneswar
10.	*The Capital Poster*	W	1988	S. Sahu	S. Sahu	Bhubaneswar
11.	*The Chanchalyakar Tathya*	F	1991	S. Banerjee	S. Banerjee	Cuttack
12.	*The Cinema Gujab*	W	1987	R. Mohanty	A.K. Mohanty	Bhubaneswar
13.	*The Dainik Asha*	D	1914	P.K. Panda		Berhampur
14.	*The Dahana*	D	1982	Narayan Das	Narayan Das	Athagarh
15.	*The Dakara*	D	1984	A.K. Panda	A.K. Panda	Sambalpur
16.	*The Dharitri*	D	1974	Tathagata Satpathy	Tathagata Satpathy	Bhubaneswar
17.	*The Dinalipi*	D	1981	Satya Mohapatra	Satya Mohapatra	Bhubaneswar
18.	*The Durabarta*	M	1994	K.M. Rao	S.K. Sahu	Bhubaneswar
19.	*The Dhwani Pratidhwani*	D	1991	Sairidhi Sahu	Sairidhi Sahu	Balasore
20.	*The Eastern (E) Times*	W	1981	B. Mahatab	B. Mahatab	Cuttack
21.	*The Friday*	W	1987	R. Mohanty	A.K. Mohanty	Bhubaneswar
22.	*The Ganabarta*	D	1994	A Bishi	A. Bishi	
23.	*The Ganabhasa*	D	1991	C.R. Sahu	R.K. Das	Balasore
24.	*The Hirakhanda*	D	1981	H.K. Mahatab/ B. Mahatab	H.K. Mahatab	Sambalpur
25.	*The Indian Express(E)*	D	1997	Shekhar Gupta	K. Ranganathan	Bhubaneswar
26.	*Info-Ad*	W	1997	Manas R. Samal	Manas R. Samal	Bhubaneswar
27.	*The Isha*	W	1983	A.K. Das	A.P. Das	Kendrapara
28.	*The Iswar*	D	1996	Manjulata Nayak		Rourkela
29.	*The Janamata*	W	1992	A. Rout		Bhubaneswar
30.	*The Janamukha*	D	1988	B.K. Panigrahi	M.R. Pattnaik	Sambalpur
31.	*The Janaraba*	W	1972	D. Chauhan		Bhubaneswar
32.	*The Janasakti*	D	1966	L. Mishra	L. Mishra	Bhubaneswar

Contd...

S. No.	Newspaper(s)	Periodicity	Year of Origin	Editor(s)	Publisher(s)	Place of Publication
33.	*The Janata*	D	1940	Godabarish Mishra		Cuttack
34.	*The Jibanmrutyu*	W	1992	Sudhir K. Panda	Surendra K. Panda	Bhubaneswar
35.	*The Kalahandi Sambad*	W	1987	S. Nayak	S. Nayak	Bhawanipatna
36.	*The Kalinga Ashok*	F	1992	—	Santosh Banerjee	Cuttack
37.	*The Kalinga*(H) *Bharati*	D	1992	—	H.K. Mishra	Rourkela
38.	*The Kalinga Darbar*	W	1993	P.P. Pani	Mrs. D. Rout	Dhenkanal
39.	*The Kalinga Mail*	E	1987	Trupti Mohanty	Trupti Mohanty	Bhubaneswar
40.	*The Kantha Dhwani*	W	1993	Anjana Behera	Anjana Behera	Bhubaneswar
41.	*The Kharpar*	W	1981	K.P. Mishra		Jagatsinghpur
42.	*The Kholabichara*	W	1991	D.R. Mohanty	D.R. Mohanty	Bhubaneswar
43.	*The Kholadwar*	D	1990	Niranjan Mohanty	Niranjan Mohanty	Bhubaneswar
44.	*The Kosala Khabar*	M	1978	P.R. Dubey	—	—
45.	*The Kosala Sambad*	W	1992	A.K. Das	A.K. Das	Bolangir
46.	*The Light*	F	1981	B.K. Panigrahi	B.K. Panigrahi	Balasore
47.	*The Lokakatha*	F	1991	D.K. Pattnaik	D.K. Pattnaik	Rajgangpur
48.	*The Lokamata*	W	1935	Nilakantha Das	—	—
49.	*The Manthan*	F	1995	Sarat Rout	Sarat Rout	Bhubaneswar
50.	*The Matrubhasa*	D	1989	C.S. Mohapatra	Pravakar Mishra	Cuttack
51.	*The Matrubhumi*	D	1951	B.K. Kar	B.K. Kar	Cuttack
52.	*The Mukta Mandap*	D	1990	Ashok Mishra	Alekh Mishra	Puri
53.	*The Nabeen*	W	1957	Rabi Rath	B.P. Brahma	Berhampur
54.	*The Nari Kalyan*	F	1993	Rina Garnaik	—	Bhubaneswar
55.	*The Nayabati*	D	1978	M. Rath	M. Rath	Athagarh
56.	*The New Orissa*	D	1933	—	—	Berhampur
57.	*The Nijukti Khabar*	W	1992	Sudhir Panda	Surendra Panda	Bhubaneswar
58.	*The Nijukti Suchana*	W	19	Prakash Das	Prakash Das	Rairakhol

Contd...

S. No.	Newspaper(s)	Periodicity	Year of Origin	Editor(s)	Publisher(s)	Place of Publication
59.	*The Nitya Nutan*	F	1991	P.K. Mishra	P.K. Mishra	Bhubaneswar
60.	*The Nirbhar*	W	1994	G.S. Dwibedi	G.S. Dwibedi	Rourkela
61.	*The Nutanbrata*	D	1988	Binapani Das	Binapani Das	Balasore
62.	*The Observer* (E)	W	1936	M.S. Mohanty	—	Cuttack
63.	*The Orissa Times(E)*	D	1965	R.P. Sastri	S. Sastri	Bhubaneswar
64.	*The Pallibandhu*	F	1962	S.B. Sarangi	—	Bhubaneswar
65.	*The Pragatibadi*	D	1973	P. Bal	P. Bal	Bhubaneswar
66.	*The Prajatantra*	D	1923	B. Mahatab	B. Mahatab	Cuttack
67.	*The Paryabekhyak*	D	1998	Rabi Das	G.R. Das	Bhubaneswar
68.	*The Rakta Chabuk*	W	1991	G.B. Panda	G.B. Panda	Dhenkanal
69.	*The Rastradeep*	W	1963	J. Mishra	S.N. Singh	Cuttack
70.	*The Rastradoot*	W	1982	–	–	Balasore
71.	*The Report*	D	1997	L.P. Das	A.K. Sahu	Balasore
72.	*The Rourkela Reporter*	W	1978	R.D. Das	R.D. Das	Rourkela
73.	*The Sakala*	F	1997	M.R. Mallick	M.R. Mallick	Bhadrak
74.	*The Sakhigopal*	W	1997	S.C. Mishra	-	Puri
75.	*The Samachar Darpan*	W	19	A.C. Mishra	-	Rourkela
76.	*The Samaj*	D	1919	Manooama Mahapatra	Braja Bhai	Cuttack
77.	*The Samalak*	W	1987	–	P. Das	Sambalpur
78.	*The Samaya*	D	1996	S. Hota	Ranjib Biswal	Bhubaneswar
79.	*The Sambad*	D	1984	S.R. Pattnaik	S.R. Pattnaik	Bhubaneswar
80.	*The Sambad Bahika*	D	1968	P. Rout	Smt. P. Rout	Cuttack
81.	*The Sambad Kesari*	D	1989	S.K. Pradhan	S.K. Pradhan	Bhubaneswar
82.	*The Sambalsri*	W	1991	Saudamini Pati	Saudamini Pati	Sambalpur
83.	*The Samayabadi*	W	1968	Sivaji Pattnaik	Sivaji Pattnaik	Bhubaneswar
84.	*The Sudarshan*	W	1989	B.C. Routray	B.C. Routray	Bhubaneswar
85.	*The Suntimes (E)*	D	1988	S.R. Pattnaik	S.R. Pattnaik	Bhubaneswar
86.	*The Surya Kiran*	W	1994	B.B. Mangaraj	L. Mishra	Bhubaneswar
87.	*The Swadhikar*	D	1988	A.K. Pati	A.K. Pati	Kendrapara
88.	*The Swarajya*	D	1991	Sangita K. Devi	Rathunath Behera	Bhubaneswar

Contd...

S. No.	Newspaper(s)	Perio-dicity	Year of Origin	Editor(s)	Publisher(s)	Place of Publication
89.	*The Taruna*	W	1949	P.C. Mishra	P.C. Mishra	Berhampur
90.	*The Trisakti*	D	1986	R.K. Mishra	-	Bhubaneswar
91.	*The Utkalika*	D	1997	K.M. Rao	K.M. Rao	Bhubaneswar
92.	*The Utkal Lipi*	F	1994	Dillip Mohapatra	Pramila Mohapatra	Bhubaneswar
93.	*The Utkal Mail*	D	1987	B.K. Routray	-	Rourkela
94.	*The Utkal Samaj*	D	1994	Prafulla Chandra	Prafulla Chandra	Puri

D—Daily, W—Weekly, F—Fortnightly, M—Monthly.

Source: Since there is no such single source locating all the above information, the authors have to collect from individual newspapers available in several libraries.

Table 7

Growth of Newspaper Publication in Orissa (by Language)

S.No.	Language	Total Newspaper Publications	%	Cumulative%
1.	Oriya	87	92.56	92.56
2.	English	6	6.38	98.94
3.	Hindi	1	1.06	100.00
	Total	94	100.00	

Table 8

Growth of Newspaper Publication in Orissa (by Frequency)

S.No.	Frequency	Actual	%	Cumulative % Publications
1.	Daily	47	50.00	50.00
2.	Weekly	31	32.98	82.98
3.	Fortnightly	12	12.77	95.75
4.	Monthly	4	4.25	100.00
	Total	94	100.00	

The above tables clearly depict that while there are only 6 newspapers in English language and only 1 in Hindi, there is a very good number, i.e., 87 language newspapers in Oriya. The circulation of daily newspapers is quite encouraging. The daily newspapers are 47, while weeklies and fortnightly are 31 and 12 respectively that constitute the whole spectrum of newspaper publication in the state.

In respect of growth of newspapers, while there were only few newspapers published from Orissa in the pre-independence era, the strength of such newspapers in the state witnessed a spectacular increase after India attained its independence. However, if one analyses the decade-wise growth of such newspapers publications, the trend of such publication is still increasing as evidenced from the fact that in 1997 alone, four newspapers have been enlisted. The real and spectacular growth is seen in the decade 1984-1994 during which, 45 (51.13%) titles were emerged. Even if, the rate of growth during 1994-1997, i.e., a short span of only three years is also quite encouraging, as 15 (17.4%) newspapers in the said spell of three years have been enlisted.

Another interesting trend of newspaper publication is the 'place of publication'. The publication of newspapers is widely scattered to almost every part of the state including the remote towns. While the state capital, Bhubaneswar, is heavily concentrated on the publication with 34 (38.63%) newspapers, the remote towns like Rajgangpur, Nowrangpur, Athagarh, Bolangir, and Bhawanipatna have started getting their local newspapers. Cuttack, the cultural capital of Orissa, remains at second position of newspaper publication scenario having 13 (14.77%) newspapers of different frequencies at its credit followed by Balasore, Sambalpur and Berhampur with six, five and four newspapers, respectively.

Besides these newspapers as depicted in the above table, there are a number of other small and medium-sized newspapers published from Orissa. While some newspapers have already ceased their publications mostly owing to their poor financial base and quality, few of them still could retain their continuity in publication amidst much struggle which include: *Janabhasa* and *Kalinga Mail* from Bhubaneswar; *Rastradoot* and *Ajikali* from

Balasore; *Agnisikha* and *Dakara* from Sambalpur; *Yugbartha* from Rourkela; *Kurukshetra* and *Matrubhasa* from Cuttack, etc.

In addition to the foregoing newspapers, some of the prominent magazines that contained news, features and literary articles have also dominated the publication scenario considerably. These magazines are either attached to the publishers of various newspapers or other publishers apparently because of their sound press infrastructure.

Table 9

Oriya Newspapers Connected with Politicians

Year	*Newspaper*	*Founder*	*Political Office*	*Status of Publishing*
1919	*The Samaj*	Gopabandhu Das (for a long period of time it was edited and maintained by Dr. Radhanath Rath)	Minister, Orissa Govt. 1940s-1970s	Continues
1947	*The Prajatantra*	Dr. Harekrishna Mahatab	C. M., 1946-50, 1956–61	Continues
1947	*The Ganatantra*	R. N. Singhdeo Raja of Patna)	C. M., 1967-71	c 1966
1951	*The Matrubhumi*	Said to be business family		1990s?
1960	*The Kalinga*	Biju Pattnaik	C. M., 1961-63, 1990–95	c 1972
1966	*The Janashakti*	Biren Mitra	C. M., 1963-65	c 1970
1973	*The Pragatibadi*	Pradyumna Bal	Ex-MP, 1972-76	Continues
1974	*The Dharitri*	Nandini Satpathy and her husband (Their son is present Editor)	C. M., 1972-76	Continues
1984	*The Sambad*	Under the patronage of J. B. Pattnaik (edited by his son-in-law)	C. M., 1980-89, 1995	Continues
1996	*The Samaya*	Under the patronage of Basanta Biswal (son being Managing Editor)	Minister in several terms, Dy. C. M. 1995	Continues

Source: Jeffrey, Robin, "Oriya: Identifying... with newspapers", *Economic and Political Weekly*, March 15, 1997, p. 511-14.

Another significant contribution to the field of Oriya journalism is the addition of weekly issues of various magazines usually appended to a daily newspaper. These magazines contain investigative articles on burning problems of the state along with feature articles, small write-ups on science and technology, film, music, general knowledge, and other entertainment notes. These magazines are so popular that the readers used to wait eagerly for the weekend to find the magazine in their hand. Although, the Eastern Media Ltd., Bhubaneswar started the trend of weekly-magazines for its daily newspaper 'The Sambad', it was spread to other dailies who started such feature as a permanent attribute to their respective newspapers to attract more readers and to gain revenue.

However, the development of newspaper as a mass media in Orissa could not be improved, both in terms of quality and quantity to an extent expected. It is due to certain factors which can be attributed to poverty, illiteracy, rural-based society and absence of reading habits and less political awareness among the people in the state.

Orissa was the least urban state in India, in which only 6 per cent of its total population used to live in towns and cities as of 1961. The literacy rate during the period was estimated at 22 per cent. These two interrelated aspects appear to be very much critical in understanding the slow, yet spectacular change in the penetration of newspapers since the 1980s.

This sort of changes is witnessed with the immediate rise of daily circulation of newspapers. The proportion of Oriya newspaper readers according to an estimate, went from roughly 7 per 1,000 to 22 per 1,000. By 1992, Oriyan circulations had gone from being the lowest of 12 major languages to being eighth ahead of Telgu, Kannada and Panjabi (PII, 1993: p. 37). The growth of Oriya daily newspapers is thus has been lucidly reflected in Table 10.

The actual growth of Oriya newspapers, however, can be attributed to strong political affiliations of the respective editors concerned. Due to some reasons or other, politicians took the shelter of newspapers and started one such media under their patronage and control apparently for a say on bureaucratic and the government. As per the estimate of Jeffrey (1997: p. 513), eight prominent Oriya newspapers have been started or promoted by politicians, especially in the rank of chief ministers. It is obvious for two reasons that (i) the source of advertisement from the state government can be easily guaranteed by the politician, and (ii) the newspaper can work as a mouthpiece for the propaganda of the concerned politician or the political party. "Those who do not offend the right persons sell much of their space", a journalist wrote in 1982. A source for the politician—publishers is not one who whispers news—leaks, but one who caught up cash (Sinha, 1982: p. 3). Such a politician publisher nexus, to some extent, seem to be a blessing for the newspaper industry in Orissa quite for a long time.

Table 10

Population and Daily Newspapers in Oriya, 1961-91

	1961	*1971*	*1981*	*1991*
Population (millions)	17.6	22.0	26.4	31.7
No literate (millions)	3.8	5.7	9.0	12.9
Literacy (% of total population)	22	26	34	41
Urbanisation (%)	6	8	12	13
Oriya daily circulations ('000)	60	90	178	697
Oriya dailies (per '000 people)	3	4	7	22

Notes: The literacy figures are based on total population numbers used in the INFA *Press and Advertisers Year Book* for the relevant years. Oriya daily circulations are those of the Registrar for Newspapers of India (RNI), which fluctuate considerably.

The trend of newspaper publishing and journalistic activities is quite rise since 1980s. Four newspapers have been covered under Audit Bureau of Circulation (ABC) till 1995 and the audited circulations of Oriya dailies reached 4,22,000 in 1996 (ABC, 1996: p. 56). Such a sudden rise of circulation and mushrooming of small Oriya newspapers can be possible for one or all of the following reasons

1. Steady increase of literacy per cent and rapid urbanisation;
2. Adoption of advanced printing technology that makes the newspapers better in format, coverage and readability; and
3. Advertiser made it easy for a good source of income so that the publication of a newspaper becomes easier.

With the changing profile of Orissa's position as an developing state in India, there is a good sign of the improvement of Oriya newspaper industry. Although the arrival of television and its wide use has been much talked about, it will not replace the newspapers. Because the demand for newspaper is a continuous one and its rate of growth is increasing day-by-day. With the spread of literacy, increasing information needs of the public, the Oriya newspapers will remain as the most widely accepted medium of mass communication for the state of Orissa.

State of Journalism Education in India

The quality of services provided by any organisation is largely governed by the calibre and worth of those professionals or persons associated in it. In order to attain such a calibre and efficiency in one's professional work or assignment, it is only proper education and training that mould the quality of services. The communication system which involves a wide variety of specialists in a wide spectrum of subject-fields, the training and specialised education at all levels and in all forms appears to be of paramount importance.

Taking this aspect into consideration the Royal Commission on the Press (in Britain in 1949) has stated that:

> the problem of recruiting the right people into journalism whether from school or from university and of ensuring that they achieve and maintain the necessary level of education and technical efficiency, is one of the most important fallings of the press, because the quality of the individual journalist depends not only on the status of the whole profession of journalism, but the possibility of bridging the gap between what society needs from the press and what the press is at present giving it (Wainright, 1982: p. 153-54).

In the present-day situation, the need for training in journalism has been accepted and widely recognised all over the world. A properly qualified and trained team of journalists is not only an asset to a newspaper in respect of the quality of news content, but also entails a sense of social responsibility. As Rau (1968) points out, "professional education in all possible forms, especially through training will provide a theoretical and academic basis for journalists 'skill', and a journalist is not only born, but can be created".

A rapid development of the communication systems and the increasing role of the journalists necessitate professional skill-oriented media persons competent enough to handle duties and responsibilities in their concerned fields. Because, the entry of electronic media, which appears to be the fastest and the most influential industry in present time, has diversified the newspapers and its products in a wider way. The present-day journalists are more tuned towards electronic media for which a specialised training for them has become imminent and unwarranted to make the press more responsive and informative.

Journalism Education Pattern

Education to formalise journalism in India started in 1941 at Punjab University, now at Lahore in Pakistan: Since then, the journalism profession has been a steady progress. Keeping pace with the technical and quality requirement of the various newspaper organisations and wide recognition of the journalism as a profession, journalism education in India has grown extensively during the last decade. After a lapse of about 50 years, the number of educational institutions providing education in journalism has also grown manifold. More than 55 journalism and mass communication-teaching departments of various universities are actively engaged in imparting teaching at Bachelor (BJMC), Master (MJMC), Diploma (DJMC) and M. Phil. level, including the provision of research facilities on journalism and mass communication at Doctorate level. Besides, 15 private institutions are also offering diploma and certificate courses in journalism. Indira Gandhi National Open University (IGNOU) is offering the latest course in journalism, through a distance-education mode.

Thus, the state of journalism education in India, however, has not been well recognised. There is no such body of accreditation for journalism courses baring Press Council of India (PCI) having its role in a limited sphere. A recently published report of the University Grants Commission (UGC) on the "Status of Journalism and Mass Communication Education in India" states that:

> the need for training is no longer in doubt or dispute, what is being disputed is the type of training that is needed and the manner in which it should be organised. Although it is true that journalists have, at various forums, stressed the need for journalism education, yet it has to be seen how far a systematic body of knowledge has been evolved by the journalists or their organisations and for training is made a basis for recruitment to journalism (Mahajan, op. cit.: p. 121).

Journalism education is normally denoted by different nomenclatures, viz., journalism, journalism and mass communication, advertising, public relations, communication, media studies, audio-visual, press photography, and so on. These courses range from diploma to Ph. D. level at different universities and institutes in India with wide spectrum of contents and duration. Journalism education is so narrowly confined that there is an urgent need for specialising the discipline. Considering the importance of communication for the agriculture Choudhury Charan Singh Agricultural University, Hissar, Haryana has introduced a Post-Graduate Diploma Course in 'Agricultural Journalism'. Similarly, some prominent newspapers in India used to recruit their staff in specialised fields like economic journalism, scientific journalism and journalist having more specialised in computer science, language and literature, law, photography, and sociology, etc., to meet the objectives of their concerned newspapers.

State of Journalism Education in Orissa

The journalism education scenario in Orissa is not much different from other parts of India. In certain cases, the situation is somehow improved and satisfactory. Orissa is, however, not lagging behind the national scene. Although Orissa has not been able to produce a national-level newspaper yet, the number of newspaper circulation in Oriya language has achieved a steady growth. As per the estimate of Publication Division under Ministry of Information and Broadcasting, Orissa has already produced a total of 478 newspapers as of 1992 including 41 dailies, two bi-weeklies, 77 weeklies, 53 fortnightly, 202 monthlies, 72 quarterlies, 17 half yearlies and four annuals (1995: p. 155).

In order to cope up with the task of producing such a large number of newspapers for a small state like Orissa, there is a dire need for professional education in journalism. Because, newspaper organisations need to be well equipped not only in respect of modern machinery, but also to a greater extent with the professionally and skilled manpower, who can better manage the newspaper and make the newspaper more popular among the masses. Another fact that contributes to the strength of the newspaper organisation is 'commercial competition'. This propels the idea of recruiting to only these people, who have got a formal training in journalism preferably in universities or recognised institutes.

The history of journalism education in Orissa created a milestone with the opening of a Post-Graduate Department of Journalism and Mass Communication in the Berhampur University. The said department started Bachelor in Journalism and Mass Communication (BJMC) and Master in Journalism and Mass Communication (MJMC) with one year duration each. With the popularisation of university education in journalism, the university authority decided to start journalism in pre-university pass and degree-level honours subjects in its affiliated colleges, thereby making journalism education more popular acceptable and recognised discipline at the +2 and +3 levels of education.

The other remarkable event occurred in respect to journalism education in Orissa is the establishment of a branch Indian Institute of Mass Communication (IIMC) at Dhenkanal. As a sister organisation of IIMC, New Delhi, it has started functioning from 1993, with a team of highly experienced teaching staff deputed from their New Delhi headquarters. It has introduced two Post-Graduate Diploma Courses, namely, (i) Journalism and Mass Communication, and (ii) Advertisement and Public Relations. Medium of instruction for both the courses is English.

Another breakthrough in imparting journalism education is the IGNOU's effort to introduce journalism course through distance education. It has also opened a regional centre as well as the study centre at Bhubaneswar, where the facility of journalism education through distance education mode is available. Those working journalists, who have not got earlier journalism education or formal training now can avail the opportunity to study journalism through this system of open education by remaining in the profession and to improve their journalistic skill.

Rural Orientation in Education

Journalism appears to be an elitist in nature. The persons or professionals, who are closely associated with the newspapers, prefer to stay at the editorial offices, which are situated in the capital or major towns. Also, most of the students after completing their course in journalism prefer a placement in cities or towns, where mass media establishments are usually located. The basic objective of journalism education is to ensure that the provision of a good infrastructure for communicators with social orientation is largely defeated. There needs a better and concentrated approach to rural communication-oriented education and training method in journalism schools, preferably in the developing states like Orissa, where most of the news usually come from villages and newspapers find their places in rural areas.

Emphasis on Local Language Teaching

In India, language appears to be a strong hindrance in our system of teaching, especially in communication education. English is chosen as the major medium of instruction in colleges and universities. While most of the newspapers published in local Oriya language, the journalists need to be more conversant with the use of Oriya language in journalism. Because, the language skill gained in the said training and education will help to develop one's aptitude as well as practice in the journalistic writings and reporting. Nowhere, Oriya is being followed as a medium of instruction in the journalism schools in Orissa. Reformative measures in introducing local language-oriented educational programmes are highly desirable and perhaps would be more rewarding in future.

Journalists *vis-à-vis* Libraries in Orissa

Culture and communication are inseparable. Culture is the sum total of the ways of thinking, beliefs, customs, language, art, music, literature, history, and tradition of a community or society. In other words, it can be ascribed to esthetic or intellectual excellence of a community. The other term 'communication' is the act of transmitting or making people known. In further explanation, communication is usually ascribed to be the interchange of thoughts, ideas, opinions or information by a systematised body.

Libraries stand between two concepts preserving the cultural heritage of a community and transmitting the information stored in it to the users for a better communication. This role of the library as the agency of social interaction brings a radical change in the structure and functions of the society. In order to affect such changes, some individuals are engaged. They are none else, the 'journalists'. Because journalists are those persons who are inextricably interwoven with the very fabric of the society in bringing the hidden facts to the limelight. Hence, there is no doubt about the journalists' role in the society and their use of libraries in the process of their preparation and developing their professional skill.

However, a journalist as information-user is being empirically verified by the investigator, which is analysed at a greater length in the next chapter. But a generalised view of journalists' need for libraries in the context of Orissa seems to be imminent to discuss here.

Journalists are social reformers, informers, pioneers, and educators of the public and custodian of public interest and social reforms. Since they have a greater role to play in shaping the society in right direction, they need right information to reflect the thought and ideas in a right manner.

Although media organisations in Orissa are quite good enough in number, the quality of journalistic environment is not upto one's mark and the development of libraries is not entirely satisfactory. However, journalists in Orissa are badly in need of information emanating from the libraries to suffice their professional requirements.

Information Requirements

Information requirements of journalists can be assessed by examining the purpose of their visit to different libraries. It is a fact that no library is self-sufficient and the newspaper libraries also belong to that category. Since newspaper libraries are not sufficient in terms of their collection, the journalists used to depend upon some other libraries in the near vicinity or some special libraries attached to the organisations or the state central library to fulfil their information needs, reading habits, and reporting skills.

Normally, journalists visit libraries to inquire some background materials, to search for a specific information, to check facts or for general information, which they use in preparing the news item(s). It has been observed that very few journalists in Orissa do acquire their personal collection and maintain newspaper clipping services. But most of the journalists do not have any such collections and they depend upon libraries of their parent organisations or other libraries in the near vicinity.

While journalists visit libraries, the nature of the information utilisation differs depending upon the nature of their duties and responsibilities. Information sources in the libraries may be utilised either for editing a news item or for writing a feature article. Proper utilisation of information resources in the libraries ensures interesting news, which are considered as assets to the newspaper organisation.

Information Sources

A newspaper library's contribution to news-making is increasingly significant in the production of news. Adequate collection of relevant information resources, adoption of latest technology and proper information retrieval system utilisation will not only improve the quality and importance of library services, but also contribute to the quality of news-making. Journalists normally use two kinds of information, they depend upon formal sources and informal sources of information.

In Orissa, the journalists' contact with informal sources seems to be more prevalent than the formal sources. It is due to the fact that they depend upon more on the records of events than that of the in-depth information recorded in formal sources. However, the acquisition of formal sources of information in newspaper libraries is not ruled out.

While conceiving the idea of building a news library, the collection of reference sources like directories, dictionaries, encyclopaedias, reports and reference books comes to mind. These are the basic information sources that constitute the collection in the newspaper libraries meant for the journalist.

However, the adoption of latest technology in library automation is an added advantage for the journalists and the newspaper organisation as well. With the availability of new information technologies in the news library and throughout the newsroom, there is great potential for change in the newspaper organisation.

Newspaper Libraries in Orissa

With the rapid growth of newspaper industry in Orissa, the information privations of the journalists as well as the concerned newspaper organisations have witnessed a spectacular change. Because, the production of news primarily depends upon the first-hand events moulded by circumstantial information. A news item is made more colourful and relevant with the background information supported by the libraries. Lou Thomas has, therefore, identified three vital advantages of establishing libraries within the newspaper organisations: (i) centralisation of resources; (ii) access to both traditional and new information skills of libraries; and (iii) provision of background information for news stories, accuracy in reporting and editing, saving time of reporters and editors, and recycling of information the newspaper has paid to acquire (Ward, Hansen and Mclead, 1988: p. 143). Hence, it is argued that the news library attached to a newspaper is increasingly significant not only in the production of news, but also building appropriate information infrastructure for the journalism and mass communication.

In Orissa, the establishment of libraries within the newspaper establishments can be attributed to the following factors:

1. Information dependent newspapers;
2. Journalists without having professional qualification and formal training depends more on references sources;
3. Competition among the local newspapers to march forward; and
4. Libraries as necessary ingredients rather than a mere formality.

When a publisher decides to setup a newspaper organisation, he initially projects the existence of a library. Although, library does not immediately grow with the purchase of machinery or printing of newspapers within the newspaper organisations, its necessity came as a spontaneous one when the quality and contents of the news are required. The owner as well as the editor of the newspaper usually decides to start a library. After a smooth start of the newspaper, the information requirement of the newspaper began to grow and arrangement for the library starts activated. However, the place of the library in all newspaper organisations is increasingly felt and the necessity is turned into a reality that ultimately helps to shape into a library, be it small or large.

Libraries attached to newspaper organisations in Orissa range from small to mediocre in respect to their size, staff and services. Most of the newspapers are small, whose circulation does not exceed more than 1,00,000 (except four newspapers). The small size of the newspaper and the proprietorship being privately managed, there is a tendency not to build a large library. Even if, there are newspaper establishments which do not have library of their own, libraries are managed by a single person in which most of the librarians are not professionals. In certain cases, journalists themselves manage the library within a small compact room. However, the availability of library and its services help the journalists to use the information they need.

Collection Development

News libraries perform the functions more of a reference library than that of any other usual libraries. The collection of those libraries is mostly confined to reference sources that primarily suffice the information needs of the journalists. However, a good collection of reference materials in journalism and mass communication begins with a foundation based on the acquisition of the standard reference sources usually found in any good general reference section in an undergraduate or graduate library. Only these specialised reference sources that are available are added to the collection (Block, 1984: p. 53). These may include directories, bibliographies, dictionaries, encyclopaedias, guide literature, etc.

Another vital factor that contributes to a good collection development is journalists' aptitude towards wider area of knowledge for which information concerning to these subject areas are collected. To develop an understanding and appreciation of other traditional subjects as well as some new emerging subjects, the libraries used to acquire information sources in economics, history, politics, literature, anthropology, sociology, forestry, environmental science, computer, etc.

Although secondary documents appear to be of paramount importance to journalists to keep abreast with the latest developments in their respective subject of interest, these do not have their places in the news libraries in Orissa. Indexes, abstracts and databases are not normally found in these libraries. Even the basic and useful professional journals in journalism and mass communication are not subscribed in these libraries except few popular magazines, which are subscribed to make them aware of the current events. The largest collection of a news library is the newspapers of all kinds, which are essential to the journalists as well as the organisation.

However, some textbooks on communication, journalism, mass media, advertisement, publication, radio and television broadcasting, photography and photojournalism, and information science are found in these libraries for the reference of the journalists.

Users

Users of the news libraries range from chief editor to the rural correspondents. Editorial staff use to consult the information sources to check the facts, refer press clippings of particular events or issues and verify the essential documents to ensure the correctness of the editorial comment. The middle-level journalists use most of the library resources. A lions share of information source are actually being handled and exploited by them. One of the vital factors, which has impressed us enormously, is the dexterity with which the editors and journalists sort through the incoming materials, swiftly disseminating between the disposable and the worthwhile (Harris, Nicholas and Erbach, 1987: p. 77).

Newspapers are generally considered as authoritative sources and any wrong or unchecked fact(s) or misleading information reflected on the newspaper may damage the reputation of the concerned newspaper organisation. To cope up with the task of citing correct and the latest information, it is the editorial staff to quickly verify the entire facts for complete and accurate news item or an article.

Besides the editorial staff, reporters, correspondents use the library for varied information resources to make their reporting worthwhile and more stimulating. Apart from the in-house staff members of the newspaper organisation and editorial-kit, newspaper libraries are frequently being used by freelance journalists and research scholars in the field of journalism and mass communication for study, reference and research purposes. These type of libraries provide adequate information/material to suffice their information privations.

Library Services

Libraries belonging to the newspaper organisation serve a limited clientele and are usually confined to the in-house editorial staff. The services which the said libraries provide are primarily confined to reference or referral. From organisation point of view, data processing is being done manually. The application of IT is yet to spread its influence on these libraries. Normally, processing of library collection remains confined within the framework of classification and cataloguing only.

These libraries generally provide information more on 'fact-checking' types of information like spelling, dates, biographical information and background information as a part of their reference services. However, the news librarians used to provide potential information sources, identifying information from other source libraries in the locality. Journalists frequently visit other libraries of near vicinity to refer various newspapers subscribed by them so as to keep themselves abreast of the day-to-day events.

Newspaper-cutting collection, popularly known as press-clippings, appears to be the heart of these news libraries' total collection and press-clipping service assumes greater importance than any other service in the newspaper libraries. The cutting system offers two distinct advantages (Harris, Nicholas and Erbach, 1986: p. 391):

1. Its subject scope and retrieval facilities can effectively be tuned to the specific needs of users, and
2. It offers very direct, and usually speedy access to the document or document replica.

Librarians of newspaper libraries maintain individual cutting files on specific subjects of interest which are frequently used by the journalists.

Role of the Librarian

Role of the newspaper librarian is not only amazingly important, but also very much crucial for the concerned newspaper organisation. But it is surprising to note that newspaper librarianship in Orissa is yet to gain proper recognition. The existing newspaper library scenario in Orissa is in a state of doldrums. In most of the libraries, either one journalist is asked to look after the library or a non-professional is entrusted the job of the library. In this critical situation, the library and its services are ignored considerably.

A librarian usually acts as an intermediary between the journalists and the formal sources of information, because, a newspaper is often considered as an information system. Out of the vast information generated in the newspaper, it is the librarian, who goes through the different news items, scrutinises them, classifies them, and prioritises the process of the specific items for retrieval. The newspaper librarian, therefore, gets involved not only in the mere dissemination of new information, but also in providing a logical explanation and the context of information retrieved. Stimulating search to answer the various information privations of the working journalists is probably carried out to a far greater degree than is generally recognised by librarians, who tend to formalise requests and expect inquiries to be refined to a manageable level of specificity (op. cit.: p. 78).

It is the proprietor and the editor of the concerned newspaper to realise the importance of the library and the essence of recruiting a professional librarian in a newspaper organisation. Unless and otherwise a good library is developed, the information-flow to the journalists cannot be properly achieved and the quality of the news items will remain disinteresting.

Journalists in Orissa

In Orissa, there is a significant continuity of several professions from earlier times to the present day. The professions like teaching, legal, medicine and priesthood reveal continuity despite their structural and cultural variations. Journalism as a profession has emerged as a consequence of social and technological revolution. The emergence and the acceptance of journalism is the result of interplay of cultural, social and economic forces and dynamics. However, the real growth of journalism as a profession in Orissa is still in a state of adagio. It has, therefore, become imminent to find out the character and position of journalists in Orissa's press scenario that still remains unexplored.

The political awakening has given birth to a breed of journalists, who were more devoted to the country's freedom struggle and simultaneously working for the profession of journalism in the state. It can be attributed that heredity has been playing a significant role in the creation of journalist. Normally, the father (owner of the press) encourages his ward to take up his path. Similarly, a good journalist seldom favours his son to take up a career in journalism. Sometimes, also the son enters into the profession either under the compulsion or to retain the age-old tradition of his father as a journalist.

In case, the father has a press and publishes a newspaper, it becomes more easier for the ward to immediately induct him/her into the profession of journalism. Apart from this phenomenon, some educated and independent bent of people gets entered into the profession either by choice or chance. Those who have chosen this profession are well educated and some have completed their specialised education or formal training in journalism and mass communication. The others have been recognised by their sheer talent, inborn quality and devotion to the profession as journalist. However, caste plays a significant sociological parameter in the development of journalism profession in Orissa, but the concept is gradually disappearing to keep pace with the time.

Organisational Structure

Journalists in Orissa work and represent different newspapers, from small to a large one and they enjoy status according to the qualification, experience and expertise and family background or heredity. Heredity in this sense can be explained that the proprietor of a newspaper gives his son or daughter a predominant status in his organisation irrespective of his qualification and experience. However, qualification and experience is really taken into consideration for journalists while deriving a proper structure of the organisation concerned.

The organisational structure of journalism is mostly confined to large newspaper establishments in Orissa. The smaller newspapers are very often one-man industry or in some cases, the owner is the editor, who is supported by a few assistants. The following organisational structure of the journalists is common phenomenon in newspaper organisations.

Organisational Structure of Journalists

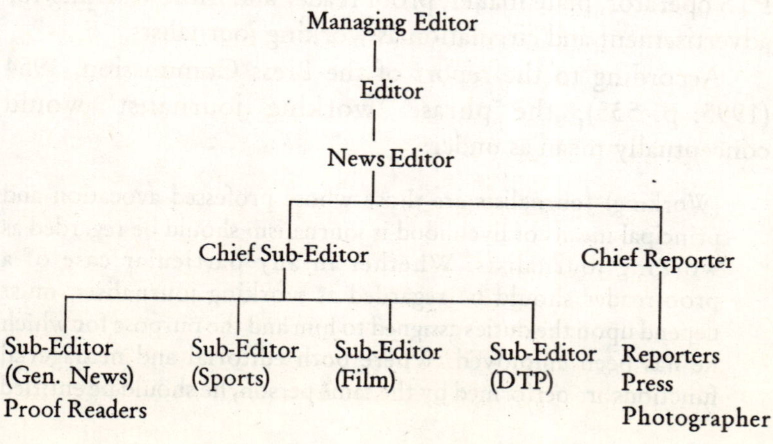

The above figure shows the various hierarchical levels of journalists working in different newspaper establishments. The managing editor is the overall incharge of the newspaper looking after the management aspect. He is either the owner or working on behalf of the owner. The editor is the superlative authority in respect to newspaper production and circulation. News editor has the greater responsibility to look into the news coverage of the newspaper. It is his pen, intellect, and the personality which bring name and fame to the newspaper. He is to see the quality contents, placement and timely publication of the news. The chief sub-editor controls the whole editorial sections working under him.

In respect to the reporting of news, the chief reporter controls the reporting section. He is responsible for the timely and correct arrival of news in the editorial section. Under his control, there work a number of correspondents, both urban and local. It is press photographer who is to report to the chief reporter and enthusiastically brings first-hand photographs to the press on sensational events.

Journalists in Orissa are more recognised, who are closely working for the newspaper, particularly those who are associated with the editorial and reporting. Even if, the organisation does not consider other technical or non-technical people like computer programmer, desk top publishing (DTP) operator, PTS operator, plate maker, proof reader and those working for advertisement and circulation as working journalists.

According to the report of the Press Commission, 1954 (1995: p. 535), the phrase 'working journalist' would conceptually mean as under:

> (Working) Journalists are those whose professed avocation and principal means of livelihood is journalism should be regarded as working journalists. Whether in any particular case of a proofreader should be regarded as working journalists, must depend upon the duties assigned to him and the purpose for which he has been employed. Where both editorial and managerial functions are performed by the same person, he should be entitled

to be regarded as a working journalist. A person, who would otherwise be a working journalist in the sense described above, should, however, be excluded from that category if his office involves responsibilities, which are usually attributable to a proprietor. But where the editorial side is controlled by the proprietor himself and there is no other employee under him, he should be regarded as a working journalist inspite of his proprietorial interest.

However, the experience has shown that most of the working journalists in Orissa in addition to their journalism profession, are some way or other associated with several other activities or practices like legal practitioners, trade unions or business or thereby they fail to give time and justice in a manner they ought to be.

Typology of Journalists

Unlike other professions, journalists are of different types. A taxonomical approach of the journalists would make one's concept more crystal. There are mainly four basic categories of journalists found in Orissa. They are:

1. Proprietorial Journalist;
2. Full-time Journalists;
3. Freelance Journalists; and
4. Guest Columnists.

A proprietorial journalist refers to those owners of the newspapers, who themselves are engaged in journalism inspite of their involvement of managing the newspaper. A full-time journalist takes up journalism as a profession or as a career and usually accepts the profession as the principal means of his livelihood. A freelance journalist, on the other hand, makes this profession as a hobby and sometimes involves himself to augment his income. The guest columnist is, however, often invited by the news media to write as and when required by the newspaper mostly because of his expertise on the subject. Either he is a senior professional or an eminent person in the field of a particular topic or specific theme.

The other factors that are relevant to depict on this sub-facet "Journalists in Orissa" are vividly discussed on the next chapter, i.e., "Data Interpretation and Analysis".

Conclusion

Journalism is a noble, trustworthy, risky, powerful and distinct profession, which is second to none. The professionals of this kind possess a very high morale to withstand tremendous role strains, problems and constraints, besides their usual professional risks and hazards. A journalist once aptly described those professionals as:

> "they are considered as public nuisance." He further added that "they are most sought after by the publicity-hungry population and the most despised by the elite involved in clandestine activities fearing interference and exposure" (ibid.: p. 114).

Though journalism in Orissa is a growing profession, it has inflicted a very tremendous influence on the social, cultural, and political life of the Oriya people. And the journalists who appear to be more devoted to this profession really contribute towards reconstruction of this society often by their provocative and prolific reporting and writing. This profession in Orissa has a distinct nature of work, which is rewarding, lucrative and demanding respect. A developing state like Orissa needs the help of such a profession, who by their fearless writing and true story reporting, can reform the society with a dynamic change not only in the structure, but also in the functioning of the state as a whole so as to remove the unwarranted maladies.

8

Analysis and Interpretation

Triumph of any user study (of a given library and information system, and a given category of users) primarily depends on a well-controlled and well-represented sample, and a well-defined methodology of data collection. The crucial task before the investigator is, therefore, to determine the size of the sample to be investigated and the methodology to be employed for collecting data. The study population surveyed in the instant investigation exclusively covers 226 working journalists representing different newspaper organisations (including the editors, reporters, freelance representatives, photojournalists, cartoonists, trainees and managers) holding different job positions in a wider spectrum.

Sample Population

In regard to identification of sample for the present investigation, a list of 490 recognised journalists of different job positions was obtained from the Department of Information and Public Relations, Government of Orissa and from individual newspaper organisations, and a preordained questionnaire (carrying eight sections) structured for the purpose was mailed to all these journalists without any discrimination. All the 490 journalists with different job responsibilities were liberally construed as 'working journalists' for the purpose of this investigation with a view to study the cross-section of samples so as to identify their differences under different variables or groups.

Out of 490 questionnaires mailed, a total of 226 journalists responded, thus having a response rate of 46 per cent which is little far from the expectations of the investigator. The investigator also personally contacted several journalists, even in few cases more than 10 times, so as to ensure timely-collection of data required for the study. After verifying the filled-in questionnaires, it was again found that some of the questions in the questionnaires remain unanswered by a quite few respondents. As these have been excluded from the analysis, the total number of responses may not necessarily be 226 in all the cases consistently.

In the process of analysis, primarily two major difficulties were encountered owing to (i) vast number of respondents with myriad job positions and responsibilities and (ii) their cross-sectional attribute on many fronts with significant difference in responses under each variable studied as a unit in a wider spectrum. The analysis became little hard, not because data were insufficient, but because data collected from 226 respondents were complex and within themselves revealed little about the magnitude of their various possible relationships. The analysis is made more depletive with the hope that it can serve multi-dimensional approaches of a reader, does not matter from whichever angle one approaches. Hypotheses initially formulated for the study were then tested with the arrived results.

Procedure Employed

In order to meet the basic objectives of the study, the questionnaire has been divided into eight sections, namely; Section-A: Personal Data; Section-B: Institutional Resume; Section-C: Information Needs; Section-D: Personal Reading Habits; Section-E: Use Habits and Services; Section-F: Attitude and Awareness of the Respondents on Information Channels; Section-G: Search Strategy for Obtaining/Locating References, and Section-H: Constraints and Suggestions. Accordingly, data analysis has been designed and interpretation is being made taking account of these sections consistently.

Table 11

Newspaper-wise Distribution of Respondents

S.No.	Group Periodicity	Newspapers					
		Oriya	*%*	*English*	*%*	*Hindi*	*%*
1.	Daily	120	53.09	37	16.37	6	2.66
2.	Weekly	28	12.38	9	3.98	2	0.88
3.	Fortnightly	12	5.3	4	1.77	–	–
4.	Monthly	–	–	–	–	–	–
5.	News Agency	8	3.54	–	–	–	–
	Total: [Total: 226 (100%)]	168	50	8	–	–	–

The present study was designed to cover the journalists working in all language newspapers with myriad periodicity. Table 11 clearly distributes all the 226 respondents under four frequencies scattered over three major languages. While journalists working for daily Oriya newspapers constitute the largest number, i.e., 120 (53.09%), only 2 (0.88%) journalists from weekly Hindi newspaper constitute the smallest number. However, respondents, who are working in English newspapers, constitute 16.37 per cent (37) of the total sample population, which is quite encouraging. Because, there is only one national English daily, *The Indian Express* is now being published in its Bhubaneswar edition in the state per cent since very recently. Working journalists engaged in news agencies like Press Trust of India (PTI), United News of India (UNI), Hindustan Samachar, and electronic media, however, constitute only 3.54 per cent of the total sample. Interestingly, none of the respondents represent any monthly publication. The newspaper publication in different languages in the state seems to be a healthy trend.

To identify the different subject areas or specialisation of the working journalists in the matter of news-writing, Table 12 primarily categorises these subject areas under 10 broad groups inclusive of miscellaneous writings. Since the respondents were asked to exercise their option in one or more than one of these

10 variables as the case may be, the total number of responses on these ten variables, therefore, has exceeded, i.e., 546 to the total number of sample respondents (226).

Table 12

Distribution of Respondents by Specialisation (News-writing)

S. No.	*Areas of Specialisation*	*No. of Responses*	*% to total Responses.*
1.	General Writing/Reporting	162	71.68
2.	Investigative	109	48.23
3.	Critic	70	30.97
4.	Feature-Writing	66	29.2
5.	Political Events	56	24.77
6.	Sports	28	12.38
7.	Films Critic	12	5.3
8.	Children's Literature	17	7.52
9.	Literary Activities	20	8.84
10.	Any Other/Misc. Writings	6	2.65
	Total	546	

Note: Since the respondents have exercised more than one option, the total number of responses exceeds 226.

On analysis, it is found that 71.68 per cent of the total responses received, did not prioritise their news-reporting in any specific subject areas, instead they do report on everything that comes to their knowledge as the time warrants. News-reporting in the areas of investigative journalism, which constitute 48.23 per cent of the total sample responses, seems to have occupied second most preferred area of specialisation among the working journalists; followed by 30.97 per cent of responses in the field of critical writings; 29.2 per cent prefer feature-writings; and 24.77 per cent are interested in reporting political events. However, reporting on films, which constitutes only 5.3 per cent of the total responses, seems to have received least significance, apparently owing to its limited coverage in the newspaper concerned.

It is observed that a majority of journalists in the state are generalists rather than specialist engaged primarily in reporting general events. However, investigation-reporting has received certain recognition among them.

Table 13

Distribution of Respondents by Frequency of Information Needed

S. No.	*Frequencies of Responses*	*No. of Responses*	*% out of 226*	*Cumulative*
1.	Daily	129	57.08	57.08
2.	Weekly	38	16.82	73.9
3.	Monthly	12	5.3	79.9
4.	As and when required.	43	19.03	98.23
5.	Any other frequency	4	1.77	100.00
	Total	226	100.00	

In order to determine the frequency at which the working journalists need information, a definite pattern of time span was provided by categorising frequencies under five major variables as shown in the Table 13.

It is found that 57.08 per cent (129) of the total respondents visit libraries daily for their information requirements; followed by 19.03 per cent (43) use library as and when they need information, 16.82 per cent (38) prefer to 'weekly'; 5.3 per cent (12) need information average once a month; and only 1.77 per cent (4) respondents use library in any other frequency as they do not stick to any fixed time span.

Hence, the above study has shown that majority of journalists need information almost daily so as to make their feature-writings and news-reporting more lively and effective, besides improving their professionalism through the use of libraries and information centres than any other means, which is certainly a healthy sign.

To identify the mode of dissemination preferred while seeking information by a particular community of users is one of the vital objectives of any library and information system. In connection to the journalists' preferences on mode of dissemination of information, Table 14 depicts five basic modes through which they acquire information. It is found that 57.07 per cent (129) of the respondents prefer to visit library personally to obtain information they need; followed by 47.35 per cent (107) use telephone to acquire information; and 23 per cent (52) preferred to acquire information through letter. Interestingly, 9.74 per cent (22) of the working journalists prefer to receive information from the libraries through Fax.

Table 14

Distribution of Respondents by Mode of Dissemination Preferred

S. No.	*Category of Modes*	*No. of Responses*	*% out of 226*
1.	Over telephone	107	47.35
2.	By personal visit	129	57.07
3.	By Fax	22	9.74
4.	By letter	52	23.00
5.	Any other mode	10	4.43
	Total	320	

Note: The number of responses exceeds 226, as respondents have exercised more than one option.

Table 15

Distribution of Respondents by Sources they Use for Obtaining Reading Materials

S.No	*Sources*	*No. of Responses*	*% out of 226*
1.	Newspaper's office/ institute's library	105	46.46
2.	Library not belonging to their parent institution	57	25.22
3.	By personal purchase	114	50.44
4.	Borrowing from their colleagues.	45	19.92
5.	By any other source	27	11.95
	Total	348	

Note: The number of responses exceeds 226, as respondents have exercised more than one option.

While one of the objectives of the study is to identify the basic sources that working journalists employ in obtaining their reading materials, five basic sources were enumerated in the questionnaire as shown in the Table 15, to which the respondents were asked to opt according to their preferences.

It is found that journalists mostly prefer to build libraries of their own by purchasing the documents personally. Analysis has shown that 50.44 per cent (114) of the respondents preferred personal purchase as the prime source for obtaining their reading materials followed by 46.46 per cent (105), who prefer the library attached to their parent newspaper organisations as the vital sources for obtaining their reading materials. While 25.22 per cent (57) of the respondents use other libraries not belonging to their parent institution; 19.92 per cent (45) used to borrow materials from their colleagues, and 11.95 per cent (27) respondents did not specify any particular source for obtaining reading materials they need. It is, therefore, evident that there is a great significant difference of working journalists' behaviour in employing different sources for obtaining reading materials.

The study has clearly established the trend that working journalists prefer to buy reading materials and to build up personal libraries of their own so as to effectively satisfy their day-to-day information needs. Thus, they seem to have a desire to be more independent in their own reading materials including texts and reference sources, which they frequently require.

While one of the vital objectives of this study is to discover the principal information needs and resources utilised for obtaining the desired information by the working journalists, they were asked to rate the particular information under three parameters, viz., 'utmost significant', 'moderate significant' and 'less significant', which is vividly depicted in Table 16. Keeping the possible information needs of the working journalists in tact, the entire subject-gamut was categorised under 20 broad groups.

It is found that working journalists seem to have considered those subjects as utmost significant that are primarily related to their professional work and image. For instance, information on 8 out of 20 subject areas like, ethics of journalists (121), investigative journalism (114), press law (106), press accreditation (103), press clippings (101), art of technical writings (98), financial market (94), and antecedents of corrupt officials/politicians (91), respectively are rated 'utmost significant' compared to the remaining 13 subject areas as depicted in Table 16. Information requirements as prioritised by the respondents appear to be a good sign.

Table 16

Distribution of Respondents by Expressed Information Needs

Sl. No.	*Subject Needs*	*Utmost Significant*	*Moderate Significant*	*Less Significant*	*Total*
1.	Art of Technical/ Journalistic writing	98	62	66	226
2.	Yellow Journalism	57	92	77	226
3.	Press Law	106	84	36	226
4.	Ethics of Journalists	121	57	48	226
5.	Indian Constitution	86	97	43	226
6.	Press Accredition	103	72	51	226
7.	VIPs Visit/Tour Schedule/Diary	68	96	62	226
8.	Techniques of Feature Writings	89	97	40	226
9.	Investigative Journalism	114	59	53	226
10.	Film Criticisms	48	76	102	226
11.	Recorded Speech of Politicians	67	80	79	226
12.	Copy Right Law norms	57	84	85	226
13.	Different Commissions Reports	59	84	83	226
14.	Press Clippings	101	83	42	226
15.	Anticidents of Corrupt officials/Politicians	91	77	58	226
16.	Govt. Policies	77	98	51	226
17.	Information on anti-socials	84	95	47	226
18.	Information on cartoon preparation	55	59	112	226
19.	Consolidated FIR Reports	45	92	89	226
20.	Advertisement	45	100	81	226
	Total	1,571	1,644	1,305	4,520

On the other hand, information on 12 out of 20 subject areas like, advertisement (100), government policies (98), techniques of feature-writings (97), Indian Constitution (7), tour schedule of VIPs and politicians (96), anti-socials (95), yellow journalism (92), consolidated first investigation reports (FIRs) at given Intervals (92), Reports of various Commissions (84), and recorded speeches of various dignitaries (80), respectively are considered by the journalists as 'moderately significant'. However, subjects like copyright norms (85), films (102), and cartoon-writings (112) are considered least significance compared to their information requirements in other subject areas. Interestingly, more than 50 per cent of the total responses rate journalistic ethics (121) and investigative journalism (114) as the first and second most significant subject areas in ranking, perhaps owing to increasing influence on nationwide movement for elimination of corruption in public life, being the need of hour. This, however, fulfils the objective of discovering principal information needs and resources utilised for obtaining the desired information by the working journalists in the state.

Table 17

Distribution of Respondents by Time Devoted for Usual Library Visit

S. No.	*Time Devoted in Library*	*Library Visit*		*Scanning the Document in need*		*Reading Documents in the Specialisation (s)*		*Reading in other Subjects*	
		No.	*Res. %*	*No.*	*Res. %*	*No.*	*Res. %*	*No.*	*Res. %*
1.	Less than 1 hour	72	31.86	61	27	30	13.28	43	19.02
2.	1-2 hours	51	22.57	61	27	63	27.88	68	30.08
3.	2-4 hours	21	9.19	28	12.39	43	19.02	49	21.69
4.	More than 4 hours	51	22.57	24	10.61	38	16.81	30	13.28
5.	More than 6 hours	31	13.71	50	22.12	43	19.02	31	13.77
6.	Not certain	—	—	2	0.88	9	3.98	5	2.21
	Total	226	100.00	226	100.00	226	100.00	226	100.00

Library and information professionals usually observe the time spent by a particular group of users on a specific purpose, so that a better system approach can be developed in the library for effective use of their information resources. However, journalists devote time for different purposes in the library, which is one of the objectives of this investigation.

Table 17 clearly demonstrates the quantum of time the working journalists spent in a library for different purposes as categorised under three broad groups. The frequency of time devoted has been categorised broadly under six time groups or frequencies, i.e., from 'less than an hour' to 'more than six hours' under three variables such as, 'reading in the specialisation, and 'reading other materials' for convenience.

It is evident from the analysis that while 31.86 p r cent (72) respondents spent 'less than an hour' in each library visit, only 13.71 per cent (31) respondents spent more than six hours in a library, which is quite encouraging though they constitute only little more than one-seventh of the total user population.

In scanning library materials, 27 per cent (61) of the total respondents spent time less than an hour and between 1-2 hours equally during each visit. Only 0.88 per cent (2) have indicated that the time spent in scanning library materials by them are not certain. However, 22.12 per cent (50) respondents spent more than six hours in scanning different materials interest to them.

Spending time in one's specialisation is another aspect that has been undertaken in this analysis. 27.88 per cent (63) respondents prefer to have spent '1-2 hours' time followed by 19.02 per cent (43) each preferred to both '2-4 hours' and 'more than six hours' in each time they pay a visit to the library for consulting documents in the respective areas of their specialisation.

Similarly, journalists' habit of spending time in 'reading other than specialisation' is also evaluated, where 30.08 per cent (68) respondents preferred to have spent '1-2 hours', followed by 21.69 per cent (49) in 2-4 hours in a week. Only 2.21 (5) opined for 'uncertain period' of time, in a week in reading materials other than one's specialisation.

Hence, it is evident from the above analysis that journalists devote time in using the libraries and a majority of them spent more time in each library visit to satisfy their information needs. Thus, the hypothesis that 'journalists spent a considerable period of time in the library to increase their habits of consulting myriad information sources for developing their writing skills and journalistic activities has come true and as such did not mismatch to the expectations of the investigator.

Table 18

Frequency of Visiting Libraries

S.No.	*Frequencies*	*No. of Response*	*% out of 226*
1.	Daily	47	20.79
2.	Once in a week	55	24.34
3.	Once in a month	19	8.45
4.	Rarely	70	30.97
5.	Any other frequency	35	15.48
	Total	226	100

In order to determine the usual habit of the working journalists in visiting libraries at given intervals, a query was designed categorising the possible time frequencies under five groups.

Table 18 indicates a significant number of respondents, i.e., 70 (30.97%) those who visit libraries 'rarely'; followed by 55 (24.34%) visit 'once in a week', and only 47 (20.79%) visit library 'daily'. This is perhaps due to the fact that working journalists are primarily mobile in their job. Surprisingly, 19 respondents pay visit to libraries only once in a month and they constitute 8.45 per cent of the total survey population and lack in their effective reading habits. The study has made clear that the rate of time frequency at which the journalists visit libraries is not encouraging.

In order to know the contributions made by individual working journalists towards feature articles, an inquiry was made. Out of 226 respondents, only 162 (71.69%) expressed that they have contributed articles of some kind or other and the remaining 64 (28.31%) have pointed out that they do not have any such contribution. To make it more convenient, the number of such articles are rounded to 10 under each group keeping the total contributions under six groups in Table 19. It shows that within 1-10 group of articles, 56 (24.78%) respondents have their respective contributions followed by 13.27 per cent (30) contributed between 20 to 30 articles; and 28 (12.39%) journalists come under the group of 10-20 and 50-above equally under both the groups respectively.

Table 19

Distribution of Respondents of the Basis of Articles Contribution

S.No.	*No. of Articles*	*Respondents*	*%*	*Cum %*
1.	1-10	56	24.78	24.78
2.	10-20	28	12.39	37.17
3.	20-30	30	13.27	50.44
4.	30-40	7	3.09	53.53
5.	40-50	13	5.77	59.3
6.	50-Above	28	12.39	71.69
7.	No articles/ not responded	64	28.31	100.00
	Total	226	100.00	

The above table clearly depicts that a large number of journalists have least number of articles (1-10) contributed to their newspapers and the lowest number of 7 (3.09%) belong to the category of 30-40 articles, respectively. Similarly, journalists who did not contribute any article constitute nearly one-fourth of the total respondents, which seem to be an unhealthy trend.

The success or failure of acquisition policy of a library primarily depends upon the extent to which its documents are put to use and how frequently the documents so acquired remain on demand. On the basis of this, the collection development programme of a library takes shape. In order to determine the pattern of use of library materials by the journalists, the several type of library materials were categorised under 14 major groups and the respondents were asked to rank them into three categories, i.e., 'top', 'middle' and 'low' priority as depicted in Table 20.

Table 20

Ranking of (Use) Library Materials

S. No.	*Reading Materials*	*Priority*			
		Top	*Middle*	*Low*	*Total*
1.	Textbooks	21	61	144	226
2.	Journals	68	122	36	226
3.	Newspapers	180	35	11	226
4.	Popular magazines	113	67	46	226
5.	Research reports	72	105	49	226
6.	Novels	52	56	118	226
7.	Poetry	38	90	98	226
8.	Humours	78	55	93	226
9.	Short stories	44	87	95	226
10.	Dramas	32	93	101	226
11.	Biographies	68	89	69	226
12.	Travel stories	51	82	93	226
13.	Scientific stories	47	99	80	226
14.	Any other form(s) of document(s)	83	79	64	226
	Total	947	1,120	1,097	3,164

It is evident from the said table that those reading materials that contain nascent information and day-to-day events are ranked top priority. As a result, 180 (79.64%) and 113 (50%) respondents respectively give top priority to newspapers and popular magazines. In 'middle priority' category, journals and research reports are preferred by a large number of respondents i.e., 122 (53.98%) and 105 (46.46%), respectively which again carry the latest findings of different researches. Materials like text-books, novels, poetry, humours, short stories, drama, and travel stories are least prioritised, as they have ranked these reading materials at par with 144 (63.71%), 118 (52.21%) 98 (43.36%), 93 (41.15%), 95 (42.03%), 101 (44.69%) and 93 (41.15%), respectively.

The views of the respondents vary with respect to the ranking of different reading materials offered to the them with varied degrees of priorities. By indicating priority to a particular source of reading materials, it is evident that journalists give adequate importance to primary sources of information compared to secondary and tertiary sources.

Table 21

Availability of Documents in Parent Library System

S. No.	*Document Type*	*Adequate*	*Partially Adequate*	*Inadequate*	*Grossly Inadequate*	*Total*
1.	Books	21	59	30	22	132
2.	Ref. Books	17	64	33	18	132
3.	Current Periodicals	20	59	31	22	132
4.	Back Journals	12	40	33	47	132
5.	Indexing and Abstracting Periodicals	6	12	28	86	132
6.	Technical Reports	25	32	51	24	132
7.	Conference Seminars Proceedings	30	21	49	32	132
8.	Patents and Standards	10	14	64	44	132
9.	Dissertations/Theses	4	17	70	41	132
10.	Reprints Photocopies	20	32	51	29	132
11.	Bibliographies	10	16	59	47	132
12.	Newspaper/Clippings	49	51	20	12	132
	Total	224	417	519	424	1,584

Table 21 represents an overall scenario of various newspaper libraries in terms of their collections as reflected under 12 broad types. These responses are then categorised into four heads, namely, 'adequate', 'partially adequate' 'inadequate', and 'grossly inadequate', so as to ascertain their degree of availability.

The analysis has shown that 'inadequacy' part of the document are more depicted than 'adequacy'. Only 'newspaper clippings' are found adequate in which 49 (38.63%) out of 132 have attributed to adequate. Documents like, books, reference books and current periodicals which figured more, i.e., 59 (44.69%), 64 (48.48%) and 59 (44.69%) respectively are partially adequate. Besides these, all other documents are found to have either been inadequate or grossly inadequate. Newspaper libraries seem to have assigned priority to maintain newspaper-clippings carrying important events for reference purposes, and documents like indexing and abstracting periodicals and dissertations seem to have received least significance.

It is, however, discerned that primary and secondary documents as figured in the above table in the newspaper libraries under survey are inadequate compared to other documents. It is concluded that there is a significant difference between the 'adequacy' and 'inadequacy' of availability of different types of documents.

Table 22

Use (Habit) of Different Services by Priority

S. No.	*Services Priority*	*Top Priority*	*Middle Priority*	*Low*	*Not Using at All*	*Total*
1.	Borrowing	80	60	49	37	226
2.	Reference	37	95	68	26	226
3.	Referral	50	60	74	42	226
4.	Latest addition list	39	32	54	101	226
5.	Photocopy	92	54	44	36	226
6.	Interlib. loan	29	69	65	63	226
7.	Newspaper clippings	64	56	61	45	226
8.	Current contents service	46	47	56	76	226
9.	Selective Dissemination of Information	57	47	47	75	226
10.	Translation	52	62	55	57	226
11.	Bibliographical service	29	61	76	60	226
12.	On-line service	39	55	44	88	226
	Total	614	698	694	706	2,712

In order to determine the use habits of the working journalists in regard to different library services, from traditional home-lending to online service, and the degree of priority which they assign on each such service, the basic services of a modern newspaper library are categorised under 12 major groups as depicted in Table 22 and the respondents were asked to rate each of such service under four different variables with different degree of frequencies.

Library services like borrowing, photocopying and newspaper clippings received top priority by 80 (35.39%), 92 (40.70%) and 64 (28.31%) respondents, respectively. Reference service is said to have occupied in middle priority by 95 (42.03%) respondents. Similarly, 74 (32.74%) and 76 (33.62%) respondents have assigned referral and bibliographical services under low priority. Interestingly, vital services like, latest addition lists, current content service, SDI and online services are not being used by more than one-third of the total respondents, i.e., 101 (44.69%), 76 (33.62%), 75 (33.18%), and 88 (38.93%) out of 226 respondents respectively. Hence, it is inferred that journalists under survey are not in good habit of using myriad information services cultivating current approach to information except borrowing books and photocopying materials of.their interest for home-reading.

Hence, it proves the hypothesis that journalists are not ordinarily amenable to current information services foı their professional acumenship is proved true.

How frequently working journalists use different information sources is very much crucial for newspaper libraries. In order to ascertain by an answer to such a complex problem, the myriad information sources are categorised under 19 major groups as depicted in Table 23 and the respondents were asked to exercise their option for each information source under four different variables with different degree of frequencies. By assessing the frequency of use of different information sources by a community of user group, the library and information professionals used to design the required information and services tailored to the needs of their respective target audience. Table 23, therefore, demonstrates a scenario of the use of different information sources with different frequencies for convenience.

Table 23

Frequency of Use of Information Sources

S. No.	*Information Sources*	*Frequently Used*	*Moderately Use*	*Rarely Use*	*Not in Used*	*Total*
1.	Books and monographs	75	60	78	13	226
2.	Periodical articles	65	87	48	26	226
3.	Discussion with colleagues	62	66	72	26	226
4.	Manuscripts	54	48	61	63	226
5.	Newspaper clippings	106	47	41	32	226
6.	Conference/seminar workgroups	58	80	58	30	226
7.	Theses/dissertations	46	52	79	49	226
8.	Research reports	41	55	67	63	226
9.	Maps	43	49	69	65	226
10.	Indexing and abstracting	34	54	63	75	226
11.	Sculptures/ copper plates	34	45	65	82	226
12.	Films/slides	27	61	56	82	226
13.	Govt. publications	67	66	39	54	226
14.	Through media reports	55	85	52	34	226
15.	By attending conferences/seminars	59	69	68	30	226
16.	Primary data through survey	45	79	63	39	226
17.	Personal correspondence	86	59	49	32	226
18.	Commercial databases	58	64	47	57	226
19.	Information intermediary	45	48	73	60	226
	Total	1,060	1,174	1,148	912	4,294

On analysis, it is found that 'newspaper clippings', 'government publications' and 'personal correspondence' are among other vital information sources that are frequently used by a large number of respondents, i.e., 106 (46.9%), 67 (29.64%) and 86 (38.05%) out of 226 respondents, respectively. Under moderately used frequency, sources like 'periodical articles', 'conference/seminar proceedings', 'media reports', and 'survey data' figure the list prominently as 87 (38.49%), 80 (35.39%), 85 (37.01%) and 79 (34.95%) respondents respectively out of 226 are reported to have used in a moderate way. The above table depicts further that journalists rarely use those information sources among which books and monographs, theses and dissertations, research reports, maps and information intermediaries figure most by 78 (34.52%), 79 (31.85%), 67 (34.95%), 69 (29.64%), and 73 (32.3%) out of 226 respondents respectively.

Lastly, among 'not in use' category, manuscripts, indexing and abstracting, serials sculptures/copper plates, films/slides are prominently figured as 63 (27.87%), 75 (32.3%), 82 (33.28%) and 82 (33.28%), respondents respectively (out of 226) have reported as insignificant for their professional use.

It is revealed from the above analysis that there is a great differential significance among different frequencies of use of information sources. Hence, the hypothesis that journalists use frequently to those information sources from libraries that are directly related to their profession has been proved true.

The Table 24 presents a detail picture of the purpose of visiting libraries and information centres by the journalists under survey. The purposes as determined have been divided into seven categories and their frequency of visit is divided into four categories. Under regular frequency 73 (32.3%) respondents used to visit to read newspapers and in this category, other purposes are left negligible. Under the second category, i.e., 'frequently', 87 (38.49%) preferred to borrow or refer journals, 108 (47.78%) used to visit under occasional category to 'consult reference tools, and 71 (31.41%) say they visit to spend time to libraries, which comes under rarely category.

Table 24

Frequency and Purpose of Visiting Libraries/Information Centres

S. No.	*Purpose*	*Regularly*	*Frequently*	*Occasionally*	*Rarely*	
1.	To Borrow Books	45	62	76	43	226
2.	To Borrow/refer journals	18	87	72	40	226
3.	To consult reference tools	33	36	108	49	226
4.	To avail their reference and referral services	28	51	79	68	226
5.	To read newspapers	73	52	58	43	226
6.	To spend time	27	54	74	71	226
7.	Any other purpose	30	54	85	57	226
	Total	254	396	552	380	1,582

The purpose of visiting libraries by a journalist is very clear. To attain a high professional standard, they use the library documents, especially reading newspapers, to borrow or to refer journals or to consult reference tools.

Table 25

Awareness of Information Services

S. No.	*Information Services*	*Aware*	*Not Aware*	*Have Used the Services*	
1.	Indexing	88 (38.93)*	111 (49.12)	27 (11.95)	226
2.	Abstracting	76 (33.66)	120 (53.09)	30 (13.27)	226
3.	SDI	56 (24.77)	134 (59.29)	36 (15.92)	226
4.	Online services	56 (24.77)	124 (34.86)	46 (20.35)	226
	Total	276	489	139	904

* Data in parenthesis indicate percentage.

Use of different information services has been not only popular in library environments, but also essential for the serious professionals, who want to keep abreast of the latest development in their field of interest. Library and information system is primarily based on these services and often considered these as milestone in their achievement. Journalists' awareness of information sources is being shown in Table 25.

In order to determine journalists' awareness of information services in journalism and mass communication provided world over, their aptitude is being judged. It clearly shows that 111 (49.12%) respondents are not aware and 88 (38.93%) are aware of indexing service. Only 27 (11.95%) out of 226 sample population are using indexing services. Similarly, 120 (53.09%) respondents are unaware of, followed by 76 (33.64%) are aware and only 30 (13.27%) are using abstracting services. Similarly, 134 (59.29%), 56 (24.77%), and 36 (15.92%) respondents, out of 226 are 'not aware', 'aware' and using the SDI services, respectively. In regards to online services, a majority of respondents, i.e., 124 (54.86%) are unaware, 56 (24.77%) are aware and 46 (20.35%) are using the services.

From the above analysis, it is observed that journalists are not quite aware of information services provided in their field. In respect to their awareness, automated services like SDI and online are even less than that of indexing and abstracting. A very considerable proportion of respondents are not aware of these services. Among the category of 'using the services' 'online' figured most which is perhaps due to the fact that the application of online system is in vougue in newspaper organisation, where a single newspaper is being published in several places through an automated networked system.

It appears from the analysis that there is a greater difference of awareness of journalists among various information services available in journalism and mass communication. It is concluded that availability of information services does not depend upon the awareness factor of the working journalists.

Use of reference databases are common among users conducting research in their field of interest. How far journalists in the survey are aware of such databases is depicted in the Table 26.

Table 26

Awareness of Reference Databases

S.No.	*Reference Databases*	*Aware*	*Not Aware*	*Total*
1.	Newspaper abstracts	84 (37.16)*	142 (62.84)	226
2.	Article first	75 (33.18)	151 (66.82)	226
3.	Fact search	77 (34.07)	149 (65.93)	226
4.	Contents first	73 (32.31)	153 (67.69)	226
5.	Event line	78 (34.52)	148 (65.48)	226
	Total:	387	747	1,130

* Data in parenthesis indicate percentage.

As it shows, a majority of the respondents are 'not aware' of all the databases, wherein 142 (62.84%), 151 (66.82%), 149 (65.93%), 153 (67.69%), and 148 (65.48%) are 'not aware' of all the databases from S.No. 1 to 5 respectively. Only a meagre number of the respondents, i.e., 84 (37.16%), 75 (33.18%), 77 (34.07%), 73 (32.31%), and 78 (34.52%) are 'aware' of databases as indicated in the above table from 1 to 5 respectively.

Hence, it clearly demonstrates that use of reference databases by the working journalists' is not a common phenomenon since, they are not aware of databases and their services available world over in the field of journalism and mass communication.

Reference tools are essential sources of information, which are frequently used by scholars and professionals in their day-to-day research and writing assignments. Because reference publications are such sources that give in-depth knowledge and adequate information about concepts, ideas and terminology in a detailed analytical manner.

In order to ascertain the awareness of working journalists on different reference tools, some of the available reference tools have been taken into consideration in the survey, which are demonstrated in Table 27.

Table 27

Awareness of Reference Tools

S.No.	Reference Tools	Aware	Not Aware	Total
1.	*Editor and Publisher International Year Book, 1987*	84 (37.16)*	142 (62.4)	226
2.	*Journalism Monographs*	67 (29.64)	159 (90.36)	226
3.	*Encyclopaedia of American Journalism*	107 (47.34)	119 (52.66)	226
4.	*Aspen Handbook of Media*	72 (31.86)	154 (68.14)	226
5.	*Journalism Educator*	83 (36.73)	143 (63.27)	226
	Total	413	717	1,130

* Data in parentheses indicate percentage.

As it is evident, 'not aware' phenomenon has dominated over 'aware' one. While 142 (62.84%) respondents are not aware of *Editor and Publisher International Year Book*, only 84 (37.16%) are aware of it. Similarly, 159 (70.36%) of the respondents say no to *Journalism Monograph*, only 67 (29.64%) say yes. In case of *Encyclopaedia of American Journalism*, 119 (52.66%) indicated that they are not aware, where as 107 (47.34%) claim to be aware of the same. A sum of 154 (68.14%) respondents out of 226 say aware of *Aspen Handbook of Media* while 72 (31.86%) are not aware. And *Journalism Educator* is attributed to 83 (36.73%) and 143 (63.27%) aware and not aware, respectively. The scenario is very clear, in which most of the journalists are unaware of such vital reference tools available in their own field.

In order to assess the awareness of journalists about important libraries in journalism and mass communication in India, they were indicated 5 libraries which is given in Table 28.

Table 28

Awareness of Important Libraries in Journalism

S.No.	Libraries	Aware	Not Aware	Total
1.	Indian Institute of Mass Communication, New Delhi	181 (80.09)	45 (19.91)	226
2.	Mass Communication Research Centre, New Delhi	89 (39.38)	137 (60.62)	226
3.	Deptt. of Journalism and Mass Communication Berhampur University Library	167 (73.9)	59 (26.1)	226
4.	H. K. M. State Library	167 (73.9)	59 (26.1)	226
5.	National Library	155 (68.59)	71 (31.41)	226
	Total	759	371	1,130

Note: Data in parentheses indicate percentage.

As evident from the table, the respondents are quite aware of all the libraries except Mass Communication Research Centre, (MCRC) which is attributed to only 89 (39.38%) journalists. The reason may be perhaps due to the fact that the same centre is more of a research organisation in communication than that of a traditional mass communication institute. However, it can be concluded that working journalists under survey have a good knowledge of other four libraries attached to journalism and mass communication.

Table 29

Need for User Education

S.No.	Category of Response	No. of Responses	% of Response
1.	Yes	154	68.15
2.	No	72	31.85
	Total	226	100.00

In an attempt to assess the interest of working journalists to receive library orientation in regard to use of different library resources and channels, 68.15 per cent (154) of the total respondents opined that 'user education' is a necessary phenomenon for their journalistic activities as shown in Table 29. However, the remaining 31.85 per cent (72) respondents do not feel the necessity of receiving user education.

It stems from the above analysis that majority of the working journalists in the state are keen to be educated as to how best a library can be used, as any programme concerning to user-education will ultimately help them to acquaint with the concerned library and information system and its several information sources, channels, and services which might be of use to them in their journalistic career.

Table 30

Use of Communication Modes in Seeking Information

S.No.	*Communication Medium*	*No. of Responses*	*%*
1.	Through personal visit to library	123	54.43
2.	Through letters by post	70	30.97
3.	Through telephone/Telex	58	25.66
4.	Through Fax/E. mail	38	16.82
5.	Through Online service	16	7.07
6.	Any other mode	30	13.27
	Total	335	

Note: Since the respondents have exercised more than one option, the total number of responses is more than the usual number 226.

The Table 30 clearly presents six different modes of communication, which the working journalists employ in seeking information. It is found that 54.43 per cent of the total respondents prefer to acquire information by visiting libraries personally as and when they need information on a given subject; followed by 'letters through post' as the second most preferred mode of communication in seeking information, which constitutes 30.97 per cent of the total response. When computer combined telecommunication revolution is on the card, acceptance of 'online mode' by the working journalists in seeking information seem to have received least significance (only 7.07%), perhaps, owing to the fact that media libraries particularly in semi-urban areas are yet to avail the full advantage of online access to international and national databases due to its high-cost-tips.

It is obvious that journalists prefer the mode of 'visiting the library personally' to obtain their desired information compared to other modes because of several reasons, namely, (i) non-availability of modern technology such as online service, Internet, hypertext and hyper media service, E-mail, CD-ROM, etc; in most of the media libraries, particularly in rural areas; (ii) lack of awareness and knowledge among the large chunk of journalists about the application of such technologies; and (iii) paucity of funds, etc., are worth mentioning.

Table 31

Strategy of Locating Information

S.No.	*Strategy*	*No. of Respondents*	*%*
1.	By scanning the current issues of periodicals.	100	4.24
2.	Through indexing, abstracting or receiving periodicals	37	16.37
3.	Through documentation lists prepared	35	15.48
4.	By consulting library catalogues	44	19.46
5.	By using references/bibliography given at the end of each article	34	15.05
6.	By discussing with professional colleagues	82	36.28
7.	By approaching the librarian	32	14.15
8.	By consulting bibliographies prepared separately	17	7.53
9.	Any other strategy	6	2.65
	Total	387	100.00

Note: The number of responses exceeds 226, as the respondents have exercised more than one option.

Strategy of locating a piece of information or identification of an appropriate reading material in-need independently in a given library seldom reflects the intellectual ability of the reader concerned. Thus, strategy of locating pinpointed information tailored to the needs of the individual clientele is very much crucial. In order to determine the strategies that are usually employed by the working journalists in locating information of their choice, the myriad strategies that are usually available in a library are categorised under nine broad groups to which the respondents were asked to opt the one(s) they prefer.

The Table 31 clearly reflects that quite a large chunk of working journalists, say 44.24 per cent (100) prefer to identify the information they need through scanning the current issues of different periodicals; followed by 36.28 per cent (82) of the respondents, who prefer to discuss with their own professional colleagues and to seek their assistance as and when they need to locate a piece of information for their reference and professional purposes. The strategy that received least significance is the 'bibliographies' to which only 7.53 per cent (17) of the total respondents prefer. On the other hand, 2.65 per cent (6) of the respondents those who employ strategies other than the eight categories enumerated in the table, but did not spell out the exact strategy being employed by them in the matter of locating information.

Searching of information sources is one of the important jobs of information intermediaries and knowing the priority of the users helps them to develop a better system approach to information retrieval and dissemination. Since identifying priority of information/sources of information for the journalist is one of the objectives of the study, it has been vividly demonstrated in Table 32. Priority factors have been divided into three categories such as, first, second, and third.

On analysis, it is evident that journalists give first priority to 'current periodicals', 'seminar/conference proceedings' and 'newspapers/clippings', which are primarily required for their day-to-day writing needs, with responses of 121 (53.53%), 104 (40.01%), and 131 (57.96%) respectively. Under second priority, 'personal correspondence', 'theses/dissertations/research reports' and 'media reports' figure most with 95 (42.03%), 103 (45.57%), 90 (39.82%), and 96 (42.47%) of responses respectively. Journalists give 'third priority' to institute's CAS, SDI, book trade catalogues, manuscripts, maps, sculpture/copper plates, films/slides, commercial databases and information brokers most, as these appear to be of least use by them. Their searching behaviour is determined by the priority factor they emphasise upon those information sources, which are essential to their day-to-day journalistic work.

Table 32

Priority of Searching Information/Sources

S. No.	*Sources*	*Priorities*			*Total*
		1st	*2nd*	*3rd*	
1.	Books and monographs	82	80	64	226
2.	Institute's CAS	31	94	101	226
3.	Institute's SDI	29	57	140	226
4.	Current periodicals/articles	121	64	41	226
5.	Indexing and abstracting periodicals	41	93	92	226
6.	Discussions with colleagues	93	77	56	226
7.	Seminars/workshops/ conference proceedings	104	77	45	226
8.	Personal correspondence	86	95	45	226
9.	Book trade/catalogues/ announcement bulletin	45	74	107	226
10.	Manuscripts	58	73	95	226
11.	Newspapers/newspaper clipping	131	68	27	226
12.	Theses/dissertations	32	103	91	226
13.	Research reports	68	90	68	226
14.	Maps	51	71	104	226
15.	Sculptures/copper plates	33	74	119	226
16.	Films/slides	50	66	110	226
17.	Govt. publications	85	85	56	226
18.	Media reports, viz., T.V., radio, etc.,	87	96	43	226
19.	Commercial databases	53	74	99	226
20.	Information brokers	47	87	92	226
	Total	1,327	1,598	1,595	4,520

Table 33

Constraints Encountered

S. No.	Problem Areas	Extreme Difficult	Considerable Problem	A Little Problem	No Problem at All	Total
1.	Finding time to read look for information	100	59	41	26	226
2.	Getting information quickly	53	97	49	27	226
3.	Getting up-to-date materials	69	66	64	27	226
4.	Locating suitable sources	74	69	50	33	226
5.	Understanding research reports/statistics	77	75	54	20	226
6.	Materials available in different languages	83	103	29	11	226
7.	Inadequate resources of parent library	81	87	48	10	226
8.	Inadequate reference services/referral services	83	89	49	25	226
9.	Poor organisation of reading materials on the shelves	82	70	45	29	226
10.	Inadequate staff	79	90	37	20	226
11.	Library services not available in the near vicinity/work place	81	55	60	30	226
12.	Parent newspaper organisation does not have a library	71	59	47	49	226
13.	Absence of library automation	96	71	42	17	226
14.	No press clipping services	62	80	48	36	226
15.	Lack of proper financial and moral support from the parent institution	67	68	70	21	226
16.	To know what type of library services are available to the journalists and where	70	59	45	52	226
	Total	1,228	1,197	758	433	3,616

Constraints are common phenomenon that every professional uses to face and which every research scholar desires to find out through analysis. To identify the various constraints and limitations that working journalists have in their career in connection with the use of library and information services, the different anticipated problem areas have been categorised under 16 broad types to which the respondents were asked to opt under four variables as depicted in Table 33.

On analysis, it is found that one of the major constraints of the respondents is 'paucity of time' as 100 out of 226 respondents do not find time to read or look for information they really need for their professional development. Some of the other major constraints which they find extremely difficult include: 'absence of library automation' (96); materials in different languages; inadequate reference and referral services (83); poor organisation of reading materials (82); inadequate resources of parent library (81); non-availability of library services in the near vicinity of the workplace (81); and many other problems thus constituting 42.47 per cent, 36.73 per cent, 36.73 per cent, 36.28 per cent, 35.84 per cent and 35.84 per cent of the total responses respectively.

The problem areas in which the respondents face considerable problem include: availability of materials in different languages (103); in getting information quickly (97); inadequate staff (90); inadequate reference and referral services (89); inadequate resources of parent library (87); non-availability of press clipping services (80); among other problems, which constitute 45.58 per cent, 42.93 per cent, 39.93 per cent, 39.38 per cent, 38.49 per cent and 35.39 per cent respectively.

Surprisingly, majority of the respondents 70 (30.97%) have agreed that 'lack of proper financial and moral support from their parent institution' is a matter of little problem for them. However, they do not face any problem under the fourth category, 'no problem at all' as enumerated in the said Table. Thus, there is a mixed response in regard to constraints encountered by the working journalists. A couple of such solutions/suggestions to address the several problems of the working journalists in the state are enumerated in the succeeding chapter.

9

Conclusions and Suggestions

Indian publishing industry in general and newspaper organisations in particular are extremely successful and competitive. There is a steady growth of newspaper publications adding numbers and value to the print media. Such an exponential growth can be ascribed to myriad factors like improved technology, increasing reading habits of the public, increasing number of newspapers ownership, and contribution of journalists. Journalists' role in newspaper publishing appears to be remarkable in the sense that the whole gamut of newspaper publication depends upon the effectiveness of the working journalists. It is an acknowledged fact that effectiveness of a professional depends upon dissemination and use of right information at right time. Here, journalists are not an exception to it. In this connection, it is assumed that the need of information for the journalists is a basic necessity, and satisfying their needs through appropriate information not only makes them replete in terms of their professional talent, but can also improve the quality and contents of a given newspaper publication.

However, it is felt that need for information for the journalists, emanating from libraries and information centres, is of great importance. How to develop an information system and provide adequate information services to these working journalists is a question that often remains undiscussed. Hence, the present investigation has become imminent.

The present study is primarily designed to reflect the magnitude of library-use in its different dimensions by the working journalists and to ascertain their information needs and information-seeking behaviour that mould their professional workmanship and character.

The sample of 226, out of 490 respondents constitutes the database for the investigation with a response rate of 46 per cent, was obtained from 40 different newspaper establishments in the state of Orissa. The job positions of respondents ranges from an editor to a rural representative having different level of qualifications ranging from Matriculation to Master Degree in Journalism and Mass Communication. Since the study is confined to working journalists only (including freelancers), it has excluded retired journalists, teachers and students in journalism and mass communication from the scope of the study.

Among other things, the primary objective of the study is to depict the complete information scenario in journalism and mass communication, wherein working journalists' need for information, use and non-use of information sources, their approach to myriad information sources and channels, their search strategy, their awareness of information tools and services, their usual habits of information gathering and use, their information behaviour phenomenon, constraints encountered by them and solutions to their problems are precisely predominant.

Results of the study are succinctly discussed in the following sections.

Conclusions

The present study has brought out interesting and worth-discussing results that reflect the information scenario for the working journalists in a developing state like Orissa. The following are some of the vital findings and concluding remarks of the study.

The study finds that 36.13 per cent of working journalists in Orissa belong to the age group of 30 to 40, who predominate the profession of journalism compared to other age groups. The trend of age factor again reveals that middle-aged persons are more in the journalistic profession than that of younger and older people. From this stand, it is evident that working journalists in the state are more in the middle-age group compared to other age groups.

The study indicates that there are different types of designations (job positions) that the working journalists have in the state. They are of 11 categories. It is interesting to note that 30.08 per cent of the respondents hold 'correspondent' as their job designation, followed by 17.7 per cent hold 'reporters' and 15.93 per cent sub-editors.

The educational qualification of the working journalists is a matter of consideration in the study, whereas it is clearly depicted that 39.82 per cent of respondents are graduates. Although professional qualifications, ranging from diploma to Master Degree in Journalism and Mass Communication, have hardly received any consideration as an essential criterion in the matter of journalistic work, it has not been completely ignored. However, the study reveals that higher the qualification forms a better community of journalists, because they need a considerable degree of intellect and academic background for the effective performance of their responsibilities.

In terms of salary/monthly income of the working journalists in the state, the study demonstrated a very gloomy picture. While almost 13 per cent of the total respondents are found reasonably paid (from Rs. 4,000 and above), 18 per cent of the respondents did not mention their salary and 7.08 per cent of them are honorary. Thus, the remaining 60 per cent of the working journalists are found low-paid. Hence, it is concluded that journalists in the state are not well-salaried or well-paid class of people, perhaps owing to the poor financial conditions of the newspaper establishments.

As regards to the different job positions, the working journalists are assigned in different newspaper organisations, it is identified in the study that the respondents those who work under reporting area alone constitute 47.35 per cent of the total response. Hence, it is ascertained that working journalists in the state are more in the reporting field compared to other areas of journalistic activities.

Professional status of journalists appears to be an important element that effects the success of any print media. This is normally judged by the term 'accreditation'. The study finds that only 29.65 per cent of the journalists are accredited and the remaining 70.35 per cent of them are non-accredited. This shows a gloomy picture of the professional status of journalists in the state.

While job satisfaction is considered as an important aspect in professional work, this study has included a point to determine the job satisfaction of working journalists in the state. Although the level of satisfaction between the parameters 'satisfied' and 'not-satisfied' appears to be marginal, the respondents are found to be more of a satisfied nature that accounts 54.86 per cent than that of 'dissatisfied 'with 45.14 per cent of the total responses received. This reveals that working journalists in the state are satisfied with their job, though most of them are not reasonably paid.

Although the sample of 490 respondents were chosen from all the newspaper establishments of Orissa, only 226 of them responded with a response rate of 46 per cent covering cross-section of newspapers with different periodicities were studied. The study reveals that working journalists belonging to Oriya newspapers are more in number (74.31%) compared to English and Hindi newspapers (25.69%). The study has further depicted that those journalists working in 'daily newspapers' are more in number than newspapers with other periodicities.

While determining journalists' aptitude towards specialisation in news-writing, the study has revealed that journalists in Orissa are more of a reporting and investigative nature compared to other eight different areas of specialisation as depicted in the analysis. Hence, it is observed that journalist working for various newspapers in Orissa are least specialised in narrow areas compared to broad general/investigative reporting.

In regard to the attachment of working journalists with libraries in Orissa, it is found that 57.08 per cent of the respondents pay visit to libraries daily, followed by 19.08 per cent visit as and when required. Again, 16.82 per cent of the respondents visit libraries only once in a week and 1.77 per cent opted any other frequencies. Hence, it is evident that working journalists are in need of information and used to visit libraries to consult library materials frequently unlike the other category of clientele, to improve their professional efficiency.

A majority of the working journalists are found to have preferred to pay 'personal visit' as mode of dissemination to seeking and acquiring information from libraries. While 57.07 per cent of the respondents preferred to visit personally to collect information, 47.85 per cent opted to choose 'telephone' as mode of dissemination of information from libraries. From this, it can be determined that, personal visit appears to be a significant mode of information dissemination for the working journalist in the state, compared to other modes of acquiring information.

The study has disclosed the various expressed information needs of the working journalists wherein it is found that the respondents have their definite principal information needs and to satisfy these needs they used to utilise resources from the libraries. They have preferred a rare combination of subjects very much linked to their profession such as art of technical/journalistic writing, press law, ethics in journalism, press accreditation, investigative journalism, press clippings of important items as their preferred subject areas, which are utmost significant for their journalistic activities and seek out information from libraries to support their information needs.

Interestingly, the study reveals that 50.44 per cent respondents prefer to purchase documents to build up their own collections at home instead of depending upon library materials for petty references. Use of libraries by the working journalists in the state is found to have primarily confined to two types of libraries although they use other sources negligibly. While 50.44 per cent of the respondents preferred to build their own libraries, 46.46 per cent of the total respondents, however, preferred to use newspaper office/institutional libraries and the remaining preferred other sources for obtaining reading materials. One thing which is very clear from this study is that working journalist preferred to depend more upon their own personal collections than any other libraries for obtaining materials they need to refer.

It is found that journalists in the state contribute more feature articles to their respective newspapers compared to reporting proper. It is evident from the fact that 71.69 per cent of the respondents agreed that they used to write feature articles and the remaining 28.31 per cent did not respond. It appears that they do not have any such contribution.

The study has depicted a clear picture concerning the use pattern of the library by the working journalists. This study shows that 31.86 per cent of the respondents used to spend 'less than an hour' in each library visit and 22.57 per cent of the respondents use to visit between '1-2 hours' and 'more than 4 hours'. In scanning library materials 27 per cent have opted to both 'less than an hour' and '1-2 hours'. Only 22.12 per cent of the total responses spend' more than 6 hours' in the library during each visit.

The study has shown further that the respondents do not have a regular visit to libraries. Rather they visit library occasionally as and when a demand for information arises. Their purpose of visiting libraries is not so encouraging. Since newspaper reading is a basic necessity for them, they read newspapers more regularly compared to other form of reading materials. Similarly, for referring journals and consulting reference tools, they used to visit frequently and occasionally respectively. Hence, it compels one to presume that journalists use to visit libraries to refer documents in a frequency that determines their specific need.

In regard to time devoted in areas of specialisation, it is evident from the analysis that 27.88 per cent of the respondents spend 1-2 hours and 19.02 per cent spend 2-4 hours and more than six hours. While devoting time for consulting subjects other than journalism, the respondents spend more or less equal amount of time. Thus journalism is an integral part of a library system.

The study has definite findings in regard to the frequency of visit to libraries by the respondents. It is found that 30.97 per cent of the respondents visit the library rarely followed by 24.34 per cent visit once in a week and 20 per cent of them prefer to visit daily. It is, therefore, evident that the time frequency with which journalists visit libraries is not encouraging apparently due to their busy schedule of reporting and gathering information in the field. As depicted earlier, they prefer to use their personal collections rather than to visit libraries. Thus, the frequency of their visit to other libraries is not very much on the cards.

It has been made very clear here that working journalists rank top priority to those library materials, which are usually required essential for their day-to-day journalistic activities. This can be exemplified that newspapers and popular magazines rank top priority and journals and research reports fall under high priority. Since these library materials appear to be essential, these are ranked in superlative degree paving the way for the conclusion that journalists give priority factor to primary documents for their use.

As regards to the availability of documents in their respective parent library systems, the study shows that inadequacy of document availability has prevailed over adequacy in libraries attached to their newspaper organisations. Except newspapers/clippings, which appear to be adequate, no other form of materials is quite adequate that makes a very discouraging feature of the collection development in newspaper libraries.

Current periodicals, seminar/conference proceedings and newspaper clippings are some of the vital information sources that received priority in their agenda for searching information.

The study indicates that journalists are not good at using current information services for their professional upliftment.

As is evident, the respondents are more using traditional library services like borrowing, reference, etc., compared to current information services like SDI, CAS, online searching, etc. This helps to sum up that journalists under the survey are not in good habit of using different information services cultivating current approach to information, may be partly owing their ignorance and partly owing to non-availability of current information services in the libraries of their respective parent institutions.

Frequency of use of information sources is a matter of great importance for the journalists, which has been studied here. It is found that the respondents have assigned priority to the use of those information sources and services, which are primarily and directly related to their day-to-day writing.

In regard to awareness of the respondents about availability of different information sources and services, reference databases, reference tools and libraries in journalism and mass communication the study has shown that:

1. they are not well aware of various information sources and services, reference databases and reference tools, available in their own field, and
2. they have the only knowledge of libraries and information centres available in their concerned field in India.

User-education appears to be a milestone in the proper and effective use of libraries. The study has, therefore, sufficiently depicted that for the working journalists in the state a well-planned library-user education is necessary to keep the library in its best use.

On the question of communication modes preferred by the working journalists in seeking information from libraries, more than half of the respondents (54.43%) prefer to have the mode of personal visit than any other channel. Perhaps, non-availability of the use of IT in libraries leads them to choose personal visit to seek out information, compared to other mode of acquiring information.

In identifying the constraints that the respondents encounter in using information in libraries, the study reflects some of the important problems. While 'finding time to look for information' and 'absence of library automation' are found to be extremely difficult problems, 'getting information quickly', 'materials in other languages', 'inadequate library staff', and 'inadequate reference services' are prioritised as considerable problems for them. Respondents, however, consider little problem to 'obtain up-to-date materials' and 'lack of proper financial and moral support from the parent institution'. Nothing is significant under 'no problem area'. It, therefore, signifies that the respondents encounter a lot of problems in using libraries for their journalistic writings. However, the magnitude of such problems vary from one respondents to the other.

Suggestions

Working journalists are those professionals, who are engaged in making informative reporting to public. They shoulder a greater responsibility to bring about social changes by their reflective writing. Their writing must be qualitative, having adequate information to support their arguments. They need adequate information to make their news items or feature articles interesting, readable, informative, and entertaining. In order to ensure such a qualitative news production, the role of the libraries and information centres assumes greater importance. Because, information emanating from libraries to a community of journalists not only helps to develop their professional talent, but also improves the quality, authenticity and contents of news items, their reporting ability and aptitude. Hence, libraries are essential institutions of knowledge to suffice the information needs of the working journalists.

This study, taking into account, the various information needs of the working journalists and on the basis of the analysis of the research responses received from them, intends to land some of the following suggestions in order to improve the library and information activities, especially helpful to the community of working journalists in Orissa.

1. Library legislation, which appears to be a dynamic form of library movement, needs to be promulgated in the right direction in the state so that the spread of libraries from the lower echelon of village-level to the highest level of state central library will be more wider and, flow of information will be a common phenomenon and uninterrupted. The journalists particularly representing rural and inaccessible remote areas will be benefited most out of such a widespread existence of libraries throughout the state.
2. A state-level library and information centre exclusively for journalism and mass communication may be set up as a clearing-house of information for the working journalists in the state capital. By doing so, the information flow intended to be addressed to the community of journalists can effectively be accelerated and utilised.
3. Library automation, which appears to be an order of the day and common place in all types of libraries today, needs to be implemented in all the libraries, those who are serving the community of journalists or attached to large newspaper organisations in the state. This will ensure effective use of information by those professional journalists.
4. As reported in the study, inadequacy of documents in the parent library system of various newspaper organisations is one of the major shortcomings. To overcome such a foible and a better approach to collection development may be taken up by the concerned library authorities through regular survey of their needs, so that availability of basic information services can be ensured to the community of journalists in the state.
5. As reflected in the study, most of the newspaper libraries do not have a professional librarian to look into the acquisition, processing, organisation and dissemination of information in a professional style. The owner and editor

of such newspaper organisation may take up this crucial issue with priority and take measures to appoint a professional librarian in their respective newspaper libraries, who can effectively build library to provide various information and documentation services to meet the myriad information needs and expectations of the working journalists.

6. As most of the respondents have expressed their desire to obtain user-education in libraries, major libraries attached to such newspapers may undertake such a programme besides incorporating some of the basic areas of LIS in the syllabus of journalism and mass communication courses taught in the different universities in the country.
7. The existing public libraries in the state seem to have ignored the collection of materials in the field of journalism and mass communication. Since they are to provide library service to a variety of users without any discrimination, they may not ignore collection of documents in this subject.
8. Newspaper libraries located in major cities and towns may develop a networking among themselves so as to ensure sharing of resources that ensures optimum utilisation of information and other library resources with limited cost and time. Such a consortium of newspaper libraries, say at the state level, under Orissa Media Libraries Information Network (OMLINET) can be set up and all the media libraries including Doordarshan, All India Radio (AIR) and libraries of the university departments engaged in teaching and research in journalism and mass communication can become members. This will not only ensure free flow of information, but will also provide a mobile character to the media libraries.
9. A library attached to an academic institution for journalism and mass communication may provide current information services of various kinds, both for the awareness and use of relevant information by the working journalists in the state. The same would lead to marketing of information among the community of journalists.

10. The librarians, information intermediaries of various newspaper libraries may bring their libraries through their outreach information services to the door-steps of the journalists so that the use habits, information-seeking behaviour, and need for information would effectively be augmented with a striking change in the use and existence of libraries for the cause of journalism and mass communication in the State.

If the foregoing suggestions are honestly implemented, the image of the existing media libraries, the working journalists and the contributions made by them, and the various newspapers they represent, would hopefully acclaim wide recognition.

Bibliography

Primary Documents

Aburdane, Patricia, "Megatrends of the Information Age", *Bulletin of Medical Library Association,* 82, 2, 1994, pp. 12-16.

Agrawal, S.P. and Lal, M., Information Needs of Social Scientists," *Information and Library Review,* 19, 3, 1987, pp. 287-299.

Babani, Anoop, Index on Media, *Seminar*, 10, 458, 1997, pp. 56-57.

Badwen, David, Information Systems and Simulation of Creativity," *Journal of Information Science*, 12, 1986, pp. 205-14.

Baggs, C., Information Needs and Pattern of Information Seeking Behaviour of Journalists and Researchers in National Media: Wales: A Study," *Current Research in Information Science*, 1993, (abstract)

Balboni, P.S., "Memo to All Journalists: The New Information Industry, *Columbia Journalism Review,* Vol.32, No.2, 1993, pp. 49-50.

Bedi, D.S. and Pattnaik, S.N., Journalism Education: Need for a Fresh Outlook, *University News*, 34, 46, 1996, pp. 7-11.

Begleiter, Ralph J., Journalism in the Information Age: Gatekeepers should Become Guides, *Times of India*, October 21, 1996, p. 12.

Belkin, N.J., "Anomalous State of Knowledge as a Basis for Information Retrieval," *Canadian Journal of Information Science*, V.5, 1980, pp. 133-44.

—, "Information Concepts in Information Science," *Journal of Documentation,* 34, 1, 1978, pp. 55-85.

Belsie, Laurent, "The Paperless Newspaper," *Span*, April 1995, pp. 9-10.

Benett, K., "Whose Job is it, anyway? *Online*, V.19, No. 5, 1995, pp. 7-8

Bhattacharjea, Ajit, "Right to Information cannot be Sidelined with Weak Reforms," *Asian Age,* February 2, 1996, p. 22.

Bhattacharya, G., "Information Sciences: A Unified View through a System Approach, *IASLIC*, Calcutta.

Block, Eleaner S., "Reference Sources in Journalism and Mass Communication," *Reference Services Review*, Winter, 1984, pp. 53-62.

Brittaian, J.M., "Pitfalls of User Research and Some Neglected Areas," *Social Science Information Studies,* 2, 1992, pp. 139-48.

Broadbent, K.P., "Information Needs in Rural Development," *Information Development*, 6, 1, 1990, pp. 49-53.

Brooks, B.C., Foundations of Information Science," *Journal of Information Science*, 2, 3-4, 1980.

Bruce, Henry W.A., "Cognitive View of the Situational Dynamism of User-centred Estimation," *JASIS,* 45, 3, 1994, pp. 142-48.

Buckland, Michael K., Information as Thing," *JASIS*, 42, 5, 1991, p. 351.

Campbell, F., "Journalistic Construction of News: Information Gathering," *New Library World*, Vol.98, No.1133, 1997, pp. 60-64.

Campbell, David K., Library Design Influences User Behaviour and Satisfaction, *Library Quarterly*, 49, 1, 1979, pp. 26-41.

Chatman, Elfreda, Life in a Small World: Applicability of Gratification Theory to Information-seeking Behaviour," *JASIS*, 42, 6, 1991, pp. 438-449.

Cronin, Blaise, "Assessing User Needs," Aslib Proceedings, 32, 2, 1981, pp. 37-47.

Cunningham, Vernonica Colley, "The Presentation of Newspaper Clippings," *Special Libraries*, Winter, 1987, pp. 41-45.

Curras, Emilia, "What Happens when with the User," *INCAE*, 2, 1, 1988, pp. 17-24.

Dee, Cheryl, Information Needs of the Rural Physicians: A Descriptive Study, *Bulletin of Medical and Library Association* 81, 3, 1993, pp. 259-64.

Deer, Richard L.A., Information-seeking Expression of Users, *JASIS*, 35, 2, 1984, pp. 124-28.

—, "Conceptual Analysis of Information Needs," *Information Processing and Management,* 19, 5, 1983, pp. 273-78.

Dervin, Brenda, "Useful Theory for Librarianship: Communication not Information," *Drexel Library Quarterly,* 13, 5, 1977, pp. 16-32.

—, and Nilan, Michael, "Information Needs and Uses," *ARIST*, 21, 1986, pp. 3-33.

Dhawan, S.M. and Sachdeva, D.C., Users Approach to Information in Social Science: An Overview," *ILA Bulletin,* 22, 3-4, October 1986–March 1987, p. 103.

Dhyani, P., Need for Library Instruction to Readers in Rajasthan University (India): A Survey," *Unesco Bulletin for Library,* 2813, 1974, pp. 156-59.

Dixit, R.P., Assessment of Health Literature Information Needs of Medical Scientists, *Library Herald,* 31, 1-2, 1992, pp. 76-92.

Donohew, Lewis, Tipton, Leonard and Haney, Roger, "Analysis of Information-seeking Strategies," *Journalism Quarterly,* 55, Spring; 1997, pp. 25-31.

Dukes, Justin, "The Future of the Newspaper in the Year 2000," *Journal of Information Science*, 1, 1980, pp. 351-54.

Duncan, Moira, "Black and White; The Press Release as Marketing Tool," *Aslib Information*, September 1993, pp. 341-343.

—, Information Management in Newspapers," *Aslib Information*, 21, 5, May 1993, pp. 208-09.

Eden, U.S., "Information Needs and Information-seeking Behaviour Patterns of Journalists in Nigeria." *African Journal of Archives and Information Science*, 3, 2, October 1993, pp. 167-74.

Ellis, David, "Modelling the Information-seeking Patterns of Academic Researchers: A Graded Theory Approach, *Library Quarterly*, 63, 4, 1993, pp. 469-86.

Farias, Manio A., Information Technology and Communication Function: A Challenge for Behaviour, *Journal of Information Science*, 19, 1993, pp. 118-24.

Farradane, Jasan, The Nature of Information, *"Journal of Information Science*, 1, 1, 1979, pp. 13-17.

Foley, K. and Briscoe, E.D., The Newspaper Library in the Information Age: A Personal View from within, *Online*, Vol. 13, No.6, 1989, pp.15-25.

Ford, Geoferry, Researcher in User Behaviour in University Libraries, *Journal of Documentation*, 29, 1, 1973, pp. 85-106.

Ford, N., Knowledge Structure in Human and Machine Information Processing, *Social Science Information Studies*, 3, 1980, pp. 98-107.

—, Relating Information Needs to Learner Characteristics in Higher Education, *Journal of Documentation*, 36, 2, 1980, pp. 99-114.

Garrison, B., "On-line News Gathering Trends in 1994-96," A paper presented to the communication technology and policy division, Associations for Education in Journalism and Mass Communication, Knoxville, Tenn, March 13-15, 1997.

Gee, Ralph, The English Provincial Evening Newspaper and its Library: A View from the Wapentakes, *Journal of Librarianship*, 19, 4, October 1987, pp. 258-267.

Ghorpade, Shailendra, Retrospect and Prospect: The Information Environment and Policy in India, *Gazette: International Journal of Mass Communication Studies*, 38, 7, 1986, pp. 5-24.

Grunig, J.E. and Disbrow, J., Developing a Probabilistic Model for Communication Decision Making, *Communication Research*, 4, 1977, pp. 145-168.

Guha, B., Documentation and Information: Services, Techniques and Systems, 1983, World Press Calcutta.

Hansen, K.A., Ward, J. and Douglas, M. Mcleod, Role of Newspaper Library in Production of News, *Journalism Quarterly*, Vol. 64, No.4, 1987, pp. 714-20.

—, and Ward, Jean, Information Technology Changes in Large Newspaper Libraries, *Special Libraries Association,* Fall. 1991, pp. 267-281.

Hannabuss, Stuart, Broadcasting Systems as an Educational Information Resource, *Aslib Procedings,* 41, 4, April 1989, pp. 127-143.

Harris, Kelvin, Nicholas, David and Erbach, G., On-line Use and End-users in Media and Advertising: An Overview, *Aslib Procedings,* 38, 11/12, November-December 1986, pp. 389-97.

—, Information Stage and Retrieval in U.K. National Newspapers: Same Effects of Change, *Journal Librarianship,* 19, 2, 1987.

Herner, S. and Herner, M., Information Needs and Uses in Science and Technology, *ARIST,* 2, 1967, pp. 1-34.

Herron, Nancy Lee, Information-seeking Behaviour and the Perceptions of Information Channels by Journalists of Two Metropolitian Newspapers, Unpublished Ph.D thesis (Abstract), 1986, University of Pittsburg.

Humphrexs, Bestsy L., The UMLS Project: Making the Conceptual Connection between Users and the Information they Need, *Bulletin of Medical Library Association* 81, 2, April 1, 1993, pp. 170-76.

Hoglund, L., Media and Communication, *Svensk-Biblioteka-Forskning,* 2-3, 1993, pp. 60-64.

Holland, W.E., Information Potentials: A Concept of the Importance of Information Sources in a Research and Development Environment, *Journal of Communication,* 22, 1972, pp. 159-173.

India, Ministry of Information and Broadcasting, Report of the First Press Commission in India, 1954, *Journal of Indian School of Political Economy,* 7, 3, July-September, 1995.

Itoga, Masaru, Seeking Understanding Beneath the Unspeciable: An Alternative Framework for Mapping Information-seeking, *LIBRI,* 42, 4, 1992, pp. 330-44.

Jambhekar, Ashok and Parikh, Sheryast, Management News Index Service: VSL Experience, *Library Science with a Slant to Documentation,* 32, 1995, pp. 95-99.

James, Robert, Libraries in Mind, between See Users Perception of Libraries, *Journal of Librarianship.*

Johnson, Karen and Haythornthwaite, J.O., Press Releases: A Neglected Source of Information, *Aslib Proceedings,* 41, 3, March 1989, pp. 99-107.

Joseph, Rosamma, How Indian Journalists Use Libraries, *Information Development*, 9, 1/2, 1993, pp. 70-74.

Joshi, Uma and Mehta, Neeta, Research on Mass Media: Trends Analysis and Challenges for the Future, *University News*, 34, 45, 1996, pp. 7-10.

Jeffrey, Robin, Indian Languages Newspapers, *Seminar,* 10, 458, 1997, pp. 24-28.

—, Oriya.......... identifying with Newspapers, *Economic and Political Weekly,* March 14, 1997.

Javelin, K. and Rapo, A.J., Knowledge Work Augmentation and Human Information-Seeking, *Journal of Information Science*, 5, 1992, pp. 79-86.

Kapasi, Heera, Librarian in Pursuit of the Simple Truth: Users Satisfaction, *IASLIC Bulletin*, 37, 4, 1992, pp. 247-50.

Karande, A.G., Areas and Methods of Research in Library and Information Science, *IASLIC Bulletin*, 34, 3, 1989, pp. 105-14.

Karelse, Calty, Mae, Information Users and their Needs, *Cape Librarian*, May 1994, pp. 22-25.

Kent, A.K., Information as Paper, *Aslib Proceedings*, 31, 1, 1979, p. 16.

Kibirige, Henry M., Theoretical Foundations of Development Information Science, *Intl. Information and Library Review*, 25, 1993, pp. 1-14.

Koch, Jean E., Newspaper Indexing, Planning and Options, *Special Libraries, Fall* 1985, pp. 271-79.

Krikelas, James, Information-seeking Behaviour: Pattern and Concept, *Drexel Library Quarterly*, 19, 2, 1983, S-20.

Kuthithau, Carol, Inside the Search Process: Information-seeking from the User's Perspective, *JASIS*, 42, 5, 1991, pp. 361-71.

Lahari, R., A Study on the User of a University Library, *IASLIC Bulletin*, 33, 2-3, 1990, p. 337.

Land, Frank, Adapting to Changing User Requirements, *Information and Management*, 5, 1982, pp. 59-75.

Line, Maurice B., The Information Uses and the Needs of Social Scientists: An Overview of INFROSS, *Aslib Proceeding*, 23, 8, August 1971, pp. 412-34.

Lingam, Pratap P., Information Needs and Use in Decision-making, *IASLIC* Bulletin, 32, 2, 1987, pp. 61-74.

Lonnqvist, Harriet, Scholars Seek Information: Information-seeking Behaviour and Information Needs of Humanities Scholars, *Int. Journal of Information and Lib. Research*, 2, 3, 1990, pp. 195-203.

Maizel, Robert E., Information Gathering Patterns and Creativity, *American Documentation*, 11, 1960, pp. 9-17.

Malhotra, Nirmal, Information Services and User Response, *University News*, Jan. 11, 1993, pp. 12-13

Manda, Paul, Information-Seeking Behaviour of Sociologists: A Case Study, *INCAE*, 10, 1, 1991, pp. 18-25.

Martin, Lowell A., User Studies and Library Planning, *Library Trend*, 24, 3, 1976, p. 487.

Martyn, John, Information Needs and Uses, *ARIST*, 9, 1974, pp. 1-23.

Mcielland, Dorothy, Transferring Seeking Skills from Education to Employment, *Education and Training*, 36, 6, 1994, pp. 16-19.

Mgaywa, Robert M. and Chakrabarty, Universal Access to Information: Problems and Prospects, *ILA Bulletin*, 27, 4, 1992, pp. 143-149.

Mick, Colin K., Toward Usable User Studies, *JASIS*, 31, 5, 1980, pp. 347-50.

Mintz, Anne P., Ethics and News Librarian, *Special Libraries*, 2, 1, 1991, pp. 7-11.

Mohanty, Manoranjan, State of Orissa Press, *Bartajibee*, 1983, pp. 42-48.

Mohapatra, Chintamoni, Newspapers for Orissa Villages: Some Reflections, Bartajibee, 1983, pp. 60-62.

Newcombe, Barbara and Trivedi, Harish, Newspapers and Electronic Databases: Present Technology, *Uliisan Library Bulletin*, October 1984-95, pp. 94-97.

Nicholas, D. and Martin, H. Assessing of Information Needs: A Case Study of Journalists, *Aslib Proceedings*, Vol. 49, No. 2, 1997, pp. 43-52.

Nissat, Information-seeking and communication Behaviour of Indian Scientists: NISSAT Study, *NISSAT Newsletter*, 12, 1, 1993, pp. 14-18.

Petter, K.M. and Peter, Suly, Information Needs of Small-Scale Indenties: A Project Study for Identies in Bangalore, *IASLIC Bulletin*, 38, 4, 1993, pp. 167-68.

Prasher, R.G., Information and its Communication, *ILA Bulletin*, 23, 3, 1987, p. 96.

Preschel, Bansara and Woods, Lawrence J. Social Science Information, *ARIST*, 24, 1989, pp. 267-83.

Rahim, S.A., Determinants of Diachronics Information-seeking among Communication Intermediaries, *Asian Journal of Communication*, 1, 1, 1990, pp. 96-111.

Renadd, Jean-luc, A Revised Agenda for the New World Information Order: The Transboarder Data Flow, *Gazette: An Intl. Journal for Mass Communication Studies*, 34, 2, 1984.

Renekar, Maxine H., A Qualitative Study of Information-seeking among Numbers of an Academic Community: Methodological Issues and Problems, *Library Quarterly*, 63, 4, 1993, pp. 487-507.

Rhydwen, David A., The Application of Microphotography to Newspapers Clippings, *Special Libraries*, January 1964, pp. 28-23.

Robert, Norman, A Search for Information Man, *Social Science Information Studies*, 2, 1977, pp. 93-104.

Robert, Stephen A., The Management and DEVELOPMENT of Information and Library Provisions in the Social Sciences, *Journal of Documentation*, 40, 2, 1984, pp. 94-119.

Robert, N., Then what is Information Science: Modelling it in Economic Terms, *Library Associated Record*, 79, 10, 1993, pp. 466-78.

Rohde, Nancy Freeman, Information Needs, *Advances in Librarianship*, 14, pp. 49-73.

Rodse, Williams B. and Rpdse, Sandra H., Human Information-seeking and Design of Information System, *Information Processing and Management*, 20, pp. 129-38.

Ruth, M., Electronic Library Systems Reach Watershed Year, *Presstime*, July, 1985, pp. 10-11.

Salasin, J. and Cedar, T., Information-seeking Behaviour in an Applied Research/Science Delivery Setting, *JASIS*, 36, 2, 1985, pp. 94-102.

Sandstorm Pamela Effrein, An Optimal Foraging Approach to Information-seeking and Use, *Library Quarterly*, 64, 4, 1994, pp. 414-49.

Sangameswaram, S.V. and Gopinah, M.A., User Studies in NICFOS: A Review, *ILA Bulletin*, 22, 3-4, 1986-87, p. 142.

Sarma, Patna, Newspaper Need a Strategy for SURVIVAL, *Times of India*, October 26, 1996, p. 12.

Sasikala, C., Information-seeking Behaviour of Managers in Industry, *IASLIC Bulletin*, 39, 1, 1994, pp. 27-32.

Schilling, Katherine, et al. Integration of Information-seeking Skills and Activities into a Problem Based Curriculum, *Bull Med Libr Assn*, 82, 2, 1985, pp. 176-82.

Schuman, H. and Johnson, M.P., Attitude and Behaviour, *Annual Review of Sociology*, 2, 1976, pp. 161-207.

Schwartz, Charles A., Research Significance: Behavioural Pattern and Outcome Characteristics, *Library Quarterly*, 62, 2, 1992, pp. 123-49.

Shinebourne, J., User Needs, New Technology and Traditional Approaches to Library Services, *Journal of Information Science*, 2, 1980, pp. 135-40.

Singh, S.N., Assessing Information Needs and Uses: A State of the Art Report, *Herald of Library Science*, 18, 1979, pp. 38-45.

Stevenson, Gordan, The Public Library in a Communication Setting, *Library Quarterly*, 48, 4, 1978, pp. 393-415.

Streatfield, D.R., Information Innovation in Social Service Departments: A Third Report on Project INISS, *Journal of Documentation*, 38, 4, 1982, pp. 273-281.

Swain, Dillip, Information-seeking Behaviour and Reading Habits of Creative Writers in Oriya: An Analytical Study, 1996, M. Phil. (Unpublished Dissertation) Sambalpur University.

Subramaniam, T., A Study of Information-seeking Behaviour of Doctoral Candidates in Social Science, *Herald of Library Science*, 22, 3/4, pp. 1983.

Summers, E.G., Mathews, Jayce and Conry, Robert, The Effects of Personal, Professional and Psychological Attributes and Information-seeking Behaviour on the of Information Sources by Educators, *JASIS*, 34, 1, 1983, pp. 75-85.

Tafti, M.A. Alai, A., Three Dimensional Model of User Satisfaction with Information Systems, *Intl. Journal of Information Resource Management*, 3, 2, 1992, pp. 4-10.

Thomas, Pradip N., Information and Change in India: Cultural Politics in a Post Modern Era, *Asian Journal of Communication*, 3, 1, 1993, pp. 65-83.

Tobin, Jayne Culver, A Study of Library 'use studies', *Information Storage and Retrieva*l, 10, 3-4, 1974, pp. 101-13.

Tripathy, A.C., Journalists' Problem of Appointments, *Utkal Lipi*, 1-7.12.95, p. 3.

Venkateswarlu, Tadibigina, Research Methodology and Librarianship, *IASLIC Bulletin,* 34, 3, 1989, pp. 115-20.

Westrook, Iynn, Qualitative Research Methods: A Review of Major Stages, Data Analysis Techniques and Quality Control, *Library and Information Science Research,* 16, 1994, pp. 241-254.

Ward, Jean, Hansen, Kathleen A. and Mclead, Douglas M., The News Library's Contribution to News-making, *Special Libraries,* Spring, 1985, p. 143.

Wellisch, H., From Information Science to Informatics: A Terminological Investigation, *Journal of Librarianship,* 4, 3, 1972, pp. 158-187.

Wersig, G. and Navelling, D., The Phenomenon of Interest to Information Science, *Information Science,* 9, 4, 1975, pp. 127-40.

Wersig, G. and Windel, G., Information Science Needs a Theory of Information Actions, *Social Science Information Studies,* 5, 1985, pp. 11-23.

Wilson, T.D., On User Studies and Information Needs, *Journal of Documentation,* 37, 1, 1981, p. 3.

Wilson, T.D., The Cognitive Approach to Information-seeking Behaviour and Information Use, *Social Science Information Studies,* 4, 1984, pp. 197-204.

Wilson, T.D. and Streatfield, D.R., Information Needs in Local Authority Social Science Department: A Second Report on Project INISS, *Journal of Documentation,* 35, 1979, pp. 120-36.

Wilson, T.D. and Streatfield, D.R., Structured Observation in the Investigation of Information Need, *Social Science Information studies,* 1, 1981, pp. 173-84.

Williams, Peter, How do We Help the End User? National Online Meeting Proceedings, New York, 30 April-2 May, 1985, pp. 495-505, Medford, NJ Learned Association.

Williams, Peny, Database Dangers, *Quill* Vol. 82, No.6, 1994, pp.37-38.

Wood, D.N. and Dower, C.A., The Use of Social Science Periodical Literature, *Journal of Documentation,* 25, 1969, p. 108.

Yates, B., Information Needs of Human Beings, *International Forum of Information and Documentation,* 9, 1984, pp. 24-28.

Zoch, L.M. and Duhe S.F., Feeding the Media during a Crisis: A Nationwide Look, *Public Relation Quarterly,* V.42, No.3, , 1997, pp. 15-20.

Secondary and Tertiary Documents

Agarwal, H., *Society, Culture and Mass Communication: Sociology of Journalism,* 1995, Rawat Publication, Jaipur.

Ahuja, B.N., History of Press, Press Laws and Communication, 1988, Surjeet Publication, New Delhi.

—, History of Indian Press: Growth of Newspapers in India, 1996, Surjeet Publication, New Delhi.

Atherton, Pauline, Handbook of Information System and Services, 1977, Unesco, Paris.

Atkin, C., *Instrumental Utilities and Information-seeking* in Clarke, P., Ed. *New Models of Mass Communication Research*, 1973, Sage, Beverly Hills, California, pp. 205-42.

Babu, A. Dubasa, *Information Generation and Library Use by University Teachers*, 1995, Gyan Publishers, New Delhi.

Baker, Therese L., Doing Social Research, 1994, McGraw Hill, New York.

Benjafield, John G., *Cognition*, 1993, Prentice-Hall, New Jersey.

Berlo, D.K., Communication as Prices: Review and Commentary, In Ruben, B.D., Ed. *Communication Year Book* No.1. 1977, New Breensmick, New Jersey.

Birch, Lionel, *Newspaper Writing*, 1976, Harper, London.

Chatterjee, Amitabh, "Library in City's Mass Media Unit, In Kapoor, S.K. (Ed.) *Library Science in Calcutta*, 1977, IASLIC, Calcutta.

Chen, Ching-Chin and Heron, Peter, *Information-seeking: Assessing and Anticipating User Needs*, 1982, Neat Schuman, New York.

Christie, Bruce, *Face to File Communication: A Psychology Approach to Information System*, 1981, John Wiley, Chichester.

Davis, G.B and Olson, M.A., *Management Information System*: Conceptual *Foundations, Structured and Development,* 1985, McGraw Hill, New York.

Dervin, B. et al. Measuring Aspects of Information-Seeking: A Text of a Quantitative/Qualitative Methodology, *Communication Year Book* No.6. 1982, Sage Publication, Thousand Oak.

Deverajan, G., *Users Approach to Information in Libraries,* 1989, Ess Ess Publisher, New Delhi.

Drucker, Peter F., Managing for the Future: The 1990s and Beyond, 1993, Tata McGraw Hill, New Delhi.

Dubey, S.M., "Sociology of Profession in India: Emerging Trends and Needed Studies", In Nayar P.K.B. *Sociology in India*, 1982, B.R. Publication, New Delhi.

Evans, A.J., "Education and Training of Users of Scientific and Technical Information", *UNISIST Guide for Teachers*, 1981, Unesco, Paris.

Ford, G., *User Studies: An Introductory Guide and Select Bibliography,* Centre for Research on User Studies, University of Sheffield, England.

Garvey, William D. et al "The Dynamic Scientific User," In Garvey, William D., *Communication: The Essence of Science*, 1979, Pergamon Press, New York.

Goode, William J. and Hatt, Paul K., *Methods in Social Research*, 1981, McGraw Hill Book and Co. Auckland.

Hanna, Nagy, Information Technology Revolution and Economic Development, World Bank Discussion Paper, 120, 1991, World Bank, Washington.

Harkevy, Michael D., *The New Webster International Encyclopaedia*, 1991, Trident Press, Florida.

Harsel, Sheldan, "Communication Research in Information Societies: A Comparative View of Japan and the United States," *Mass Communication Review Year Book*, Vol. 2, 1981, In Wilhait, C. Clevlard, Sage, Thousand Oak.

India, Ministry of Information and Broadcasting, *Press in India*, 1993, Publication Division, New Delhi.

India, Ministry of Information and Broadcasting, *Mass Media in India*, 1995, Publication Division, New Delhi.

Joseph, Rosamma, A Study of Libraries, Information Needs and Use of Information Sciences in Newspaper Establishment in Kerala, Unpublished Ph.D. thesis, 1990, University of Calicut.

Katz, William A., Introduction to Reference Work, V.I. 1982, McGraw Hill, New York.

Kawatra, P.S., *Library User Studies*, 1992, Jaico Publishers House Bombay, p. 100.

Kawatra, P.S., *Fundamentals of Documentation*, 1989, Sterling Publication, Delhi.

Kent, Allen, Library User Studies, *Encyclopaedia of Library and Information Science*, Vol.45, pp. 147-156.

Khanna, J.K., *Advances in Librarianship*, 1985, Ess Ess Publishers, New Delhi.

Klapper, Joseph T., *The Effectiveness of Mass Media*, In Grabber, Davis A. Ed. *Media Power in Politics*, 1990, MacMillan India, New Delhi.

Koblitz, J., *Librarianship and Documentation Information: Distinctive Features and Common Aspects, In On Theoretical Problem in Informatics*, 1969, All Institute for Scientific and Technological Information, Moscow.

Kumar, Girija, *Library Development in India*, 1989, Vikas, New Delhi, p. 253.

—, *Defining the Concept of Information Needs*, In Binwal, J.C., Chandel, A.S. and Saraf, Veena, Ed. *Social Science Information: Problems and Prospects*, 1990, Har Anand, New Delhi, pp. 253-71.

Kumar, Krishna, *Research Libraries in Developing Countries*, 1992, Vikas Publishing House, New Delhi.

Kumar, Krishna, *Reference Science*, 1978, Vikas, New Delhi.

Lang, Kurt, *Study of Communications*, In Barnaun, K. et al. Ed. *International Encyclopaedia of Communication*, Vol.1. 1989, Oxford University Press, NewYork.

Lazer, Peter, Information System Design and Management, 1985, Sarada Ranganathan Endowment, Bangalore.

Lindzey, Gondnor and Aronson, Ellict, *The Handbook of Social Psychology*, 1968, Arnold Pub. Co., New Delhi, p. 321.

Macbride, Sean, *Many Voices, One World: Communication and Society, Today and Tomorrow*, 1980, Kasen and Rage, London.

Mahajan, K., *Communication and Society*, 1990, Classical Publication, New Delhi.

Maheswarppa, B.S and Hiremath, C.M., *Information User Pattern of Social Scientists in a University Environment in India*, In Raju, A.A.N. Ed. *New Vistas in Library and Information Science*, 1995, Vikas, New Delhi, p. 293.

Mansingh, Mayadhar, *History of Oriya Literature*, 1962, New Delhi.

Manson, R.U., Manson, F.M. and Culnan, M.J., *Ethics of Information Management*, 1995, Sage Publication, Thousand Oak.

Menon, Vijay, *Regional Cooperation and Mass Communication Information in Asia: Role of Amic*, In Gupta B.M. Ed. *Handbook Libraries. Archives and Information Centres in India,* 1987, pp. 267-73.

Mikkilesan, Britha, *Methods of Development Work and Research*, 1995, Sage Publication, New Delhi.

Mohsin, S.M., *Research Methods on Behaviour Sciences,* 1984, Orient Longman, Calcutta.

Nachmias, David and Nachmias, Chava, *Research Methods in the Social Science*, 1981, St.Martin's Press, New York.

Naidu, M.K.R., *Information need of Social Scientists in India: UGC Information Centre for Social Scientists*, In Binwal, J.C., Chandel, A.L. and Saraf, Veena, Ed. *Social Science Information: Problems and Prospects*, 1990, Har-Anand, New Delhi, pp. 346-53.

Nanun, Burt, *User Needs for Improvement in the year 2000*, In Boaz, Maltha, *Strategies for Meeting the Information Needs of Society in the Year 2000*, 1981, Libraries United Inc. little Colorado.

Padhi, K.S. and Sahu, R.M., *The Press in India: Perspective in Development and Relevance*, 1997, Kaniska Publications, New Delhi.

Paisley, W. and Hardy A., *Information and Work: Research on the Improvement of Practitioner Information System*, 1980, Stanford University, Stanford CA.

Parthasarathi R., *Basic Journalism*, 1984, Macmillan, New Delhi.

—, *Journalism in India*: *From the Earliest Time to the Present Day*, 3rd Ed, 1995, Sterling Publisher, New Delhi.

Porter, William E., *Journalism*, In Silis, K.M. *International Encyclopaedia of Social Science*, 1968, Macmillan and Free Press, London.

Prasad, H.N., *Information Needs and Uses*, 1992, Indian Bibliography Centre, Varanasi, pp. 80-81.

Prasher, R.G., *Information and its Communication*, 1991, Medallm Press, New Delhi.

Rau, M.C., *The Press in India*, 1968, Allied Publishers, New Delhi.

Runkel, P.J. and McGrath, J.E., *Research in Human Behaviour*, 1972, Holt Rinehart and Winston Inc. New York.

Samal, J.K., *History of Modern Orissa*, 1984, Firm K L M. Calcutta.

Saracevik, K., *Instrumental Utilities and Information Seeking, In New Needs for Mass Communication Research*, 1983, Sage Publication, Beverly Hills.

Saracevik, T., *Introduction to Information Science*, 1970, Bowker, New York.

Saraf, Veena, Binwal, J.C., and Misra, R., *Information-seeking Behaviour of Research in North-Eastern India: Case Study of NEHU and Manipur University,* In Binwal J.C., Chandel, A.S. and Saraf, Veena. Ed. *Social Science Information: Problems and Prospects,* 1990, Har Anand, New Delhi, pp. 354-62.

Satish, N.G., *Attitude Towards Information: A Study of Social Scientists*, 1994, Concept, New Delhi.

Sinha, Arun, *The Indian Express Magazine*, January 24, 1982, p. 3.

Sharma, S.R. and Chaturvedi, Anil, *Future of Mass Communication*, 1996, Radha Publication, New Delhi.

Shera, J.H., *Sociological Foundations of Librarianship:* Asia Publishing House, New York.

Shera, J.H., *The Foundation of Education for Librarianship*, 1992, Becker and Haley, New York.

Sindwani, Trilok N., *Newspaper Economics and Management*, 1979, Ajanta, New Delhi.

Skinner, B.F., *About Behaviourism*, 1974, Penguin Books, London.

Stevans, Norman D., *The History of Information*, In Simonton, Wesley, Ed. *Advance in Librarianship*, Vol.14, 1996, Academic Press, Orlando.

Synder, Louis L., *Journalism*, In Emind, Ed. *Encyclopaedia*, Vol.16, 1973.

Sypher, H.E. and Applecate, J.L., *Organising Communication Behaviour*, The *Role of Schema and Construct*, In Bosteom, Robert W. Ed. *Communication Year Book* No.8. 1984, Sage Publication, Beverly Hill.

Talero, Eduardo and Gaudette, Philip, *Harnessing Information for Development*, A proposal for a World Bank Group Strategy: World Bank Discussion Paper, 1996, World Bank, Washington.

Toffler, Alvin, *Future Shocks*, 1990, Bantham Books, New York.

Tripathy, S.C., *Development of Newspaper and Journalism in Orissa*, 1990, Orissa Book Store, Cuttack.

Unesco, *Guidelines on Studies of Information Users,* Unesco, 1981.

Vilanilam, J.V., *Science, Communication and Development*, 1993, Sage Publications, New Delhi.

Wainwright, David, *Journalism Made Simple*, 1992, Rupa and Co., Calcutta.

Webster, N., *Third New International Dictionary*, 1978, Maniam, Massachusetts, p. 116.

William, William, F., *Principle of Automated Retrieval*, 1965, Business Press, Illinois.

Zijp, W., *Improving the Transfer and Use of Agriculture Information: A Guide to Information Technology*: World Bank Discussion Paper, 1994, World Bank, Washington.

Index